Praise for *The Life of Dad*

"When I found out I was going to be a dad I thought, 'Can I handle it? Would I hopefully be like my dad? What would my kids be like?' Then I felt pride and love. It was terrifying and amazing. Just like it is for every new dad. Reading *The Life of Dad* will help you relax and know that it's worked out for all these amazing dads, and it'll work out for you."

—Mark Cuban, entrepreneur, Dallas Mavericks owner, *Shark Tank* star

"Becoming a dad doesn't come with an instruction book. Or at least it never did before now. Jon Finkel and Art Eddy have packed these 256 pages with wit and wisdom from world-class superdads and distilled their real-world experience into actionable, easily digestible advice. Whenever new dads ask what to expect, the hardest part is figuring out where even to begin. Now I can point them toward a copy of *The Life of Dad*.

—Robert Irvine, celebrity chef, philanthropist, father of two

"I was happy to chat with the crew here at Life of Dad a while back and share all sides of fatherhood with them. There is a saying that it takes a village to raise a child. With this book you can use the wisdom from all of these dads to help you raise your children. If you put in the time and love your children, it will come back tenfold. Fatherhood is a rewarding journey that I can say I am proud to be on. Make sure you keep on living that Life of Dad!"

—Jim Kelly, Pro Football Hall of Fame quarterback

"Dads don't stop for directions, read assembly instructions, or consult the owner's manual. But everything a dad needs to know is in here. *The Life of Dad* contains the collected wisdom, knowledge, and love of countless fathers. If you are a dad, have a dad, or ever hope to be a dad, read this book."

—Steve Rushin, bestselling author, National Sportswriter of the Year winner

"During my career I was fortunate to be surrounded by so many people I considered to be high-character, high-integrity people, like Steelers head coach Chuck Noll. *The Life of Dad* is filled cover-to-cover with the same types of men offering excellent thoughts and stories about fatherhood. It's a great playbook for dads."

—"Mean" Joe Greene, NFL and College Football Hall of Famer,
four-time Super Bowl champion

Praise for *The Life of Dad*

"When my kids were younger, we would sit down for dinner and I would ask them, 'Tell me one thing you did for your brain and one thing you did for your body today?' I wanted to be aware of how they took care of themselves mentally *and* physically, and to never take it for granted. I felt that if they had to articulate it, that would make them more aware, more present. I think brain-and-body balance is key. One thing you can do for your brain as a father is to read *The Life of Dad*, absorb the knowledge of all the great dads inside, and work on being better every day. And then you can do some push-ups, crunches, and squats."

—Gunnar Peterson, Los Angeles Lakers director of strength and endurance, top Beverly Hills trainer, entrepreneur

"There has been nothing else in my life that has given me the utter satisfaction and joy that raising my daughters with my amazing wife has given me. It's a lot of fun to learn from others how they have managed to deal with raising kids in somewhat unique situations that were caused by the career paths and success of the fathers. And it's even more fun to see that no matter who you are, you can have a lot of the same joys, hurdles, frustrations, and failures that every dad goes through. *The Life of Dad* should be a must-read for any dad who's been through it all or is about to get started on this wonderful journey that is fatherhood."

—James Blake, former professional tennis player, *New York Times* bestselling author, proud husband and father, founder of The James Blake Foundation

"My two passions in this world are being a dad and basketball. Just like having a coach helps you get better on the court, reading *The Life of Dad* will help you learn new things about being a better father. I know I did."

—Nate Robinson, BIG3 star, three-time NBA Slam Dunk champion

Priceless Dad Advice from Michael Strahan, k Hamill, Jim Gaffigan, Mark Cuban, and M

The

LIFE of
DAD

Reflections on Fatherhood from Today's Leaders, Icons, and Legendary Dads

JON FINKEL and ART EDDY
From the Popular Podcast *The Life of Dad Show*

Adams Media
New York London Toronto Sydney New Delhi

Aadamsmedia

Adams Media
An Imprint of Simon & Schuster, Inc.
57 Littlefield Street
Avon, Massachusetts 02322

First Adams Media hardcover edition May 2019

ADAMS MEDIA and colophon are trademarks of Simon & Schuster.

For information about special discounts for bulk purchases, please contact Simon & Schuster Special Sales at 1-866-506-1949 or business@simonandschuster.com.

The Simon & Schuster Speakers Bureau can bring authors to your live event. For more information or to book an event contact the Simon & Schuster Speakers Bureau at 1-866-248-3049 or visit our website at www.simonspeakers.com.

Interior design by Michelle Kelly

Manufactured in the United States of America

10   9   8   7   6   5   4   3   2   1

Library of Congress Cataloging-in-Publication Data
Names: Finkel, Jon, author. | Eddy, Art, author.
Title: The life of dad / Jon Finkel and Art Eddy, from the popular podcast The Life of Dad Show.
Description: Avon, Massachusetts: Adams Media, 2019.
Includes index.
Identifiers: LCCN 2018058485 | ISBN 9781721400300 (hc) | ISBN 9781721400317 (ebook)
Subjects: LCSH: Fatherhood. | Fathers.
Classification: LCC HQ756 .F54 2019 | DDC 306.874/2--dc23
LC record available at https://lccn.loc.gov/2018058485

ISBN 978-1-72140-030-0
ISBN 978-1-72140-031-7 (ebook)

Contents

Acknowledgments

I've spent the better part of a year conducting interviews, writing, and compiling stories, strategies, and skills from world-class dads, but I'd like to dedicate this book to the one world-class father I talk to almost every day: my own. I can confidently say that this book would not be here without him (and not for the obvious biological reasons). I moved to Los Angeles right after college to pursue some kind of writing career, and within a few months my old college desktop computer died on me and I couldn't afford a new one. After working as a production assistant all day, I would go to the Santa Monica Public Library at night to use their free computers to get my writing done and to check and send emails looking for writing assignments.

One night I got back to my apartment and saw a package waiting for me. I opened it, and it was a brand-new Dell laptop with a note from my dad: "I believe in you. You can't be a writer without something to write on, so go write something great. Love, Dad & Mom."

That was several laptops and several books ago, but the support my parents showed me and their belief in me is exactly what I strive to do for my own kids.

On that note, this book is also dedicated to my partner in the front seat of this *Life of Dad* family road trip, my wife Steph, and the two kids screaming in the back, Reese and Grant. (No, we're not there yet… Stop asking.)

—Jon

How did I get here?

I never thought in a million years that I would be an author of a book, especially one on fatherhood. Growing up, I wanted to be a running back in the NFL or an astronaut. Not once did I ever think that I would be writing about being a dad. Yet as the cliché states, a baby changes everything. When my wife gave birth to our first daughter, my career in radio took a backseat. When my youngest was born, I became a stay-at-home dad. Little did I know that would spark a career for me that would change my life.

I started working for *Life of Dad*, sharing my thoughts on fatherhood. Next I began to interview other dads and ask them how becoming a father changed their lives. That brought about *The Life of Dad Show*. From that podcast came this book. I am very excited to share this collection of essays from other dads talking about the most important thing in their lives: their kids.

This book is dedicated to my parents, Art and Judy; my wife, Jessica; and my daughters, Lily and Jordan. Thanks for believing in me.

—Art

About *Life of Dad*

Back when this book was just a twinkle in our eyes, we started gathering parenting advice in our "My Life of Dad" column on the *Life of Dad* website, which eventually became *The Life of Dad Show* podcast.

Our very first installment was with "The Fonz" himself, Henry Winkler, who is featured in this book. While Winkler was the most famous TV actor of his generation, he is also famous in Hollywood for two other things: being an extraordinarily nice guy and being a family man—two traits we can absolutely get behind here at LOD.

Since that interview, we've recorded more than three hundred episodes of *The Life of Dad Show* with as many leaders, luminaries, and legendary dads that we could find. Along the way, our online community of fathers has grown to over two million strong and has become a home for dads to connect, comment, laugh, and share their thoughts on parenting. With each new interview and conversation, our collective knowledge grew to the point where we felt the next natural step was to put it all in one place, which leads to the book in your hands.

Introduction:
Don't Skim This Part

"There are many kinds of success in life worth having....But for unflagging interest and enjoyment, a household of children, if things go reasonably well, certainly makes all other forms of success and achievement lose their importance by comparison."
—Theodore Roosevelt, Father of Six

"And just remember, the best thing about kids...is making them!"
—Thornton Melon (Rodney Dangerfield), *Back to School*

We don't know you personally, but we know this: You want to be an awesome dad. Well, here's a hint, if you want to be an awesome dad, then you likely already are. In fact, reading this book is proof. You've opened your mind to getting better at the most important responsibility you have in this world and for that we applaud you. We're also here to help.

For the better part of the last decade, we've built up the *Life of Dad* community from a starting point of zero to over two million fans on *Facebook* and our signature *The Life of Dad Show* podcast, with more than 600k downloads. During this time, we've interviewed more than one hundred leaders, icons, and legendary fathers from the worlds of business, sports, entertainment, literature, the military, and many more. In essence, we've created a veritable "*Google* for dads." Alas, we don't have the luxury of a search bar and timely doodles, so we've divided *The Life of Dad* into three parts, each representing a different facet of fatherhood.

Part I is titled Tools and this section focuses on a series of core traits (positive mindset, character, work ethic, humility, values, and wisdom) that dads try to instill in their children, along with advice on how to do so from NFL Hall of Famers, Grammy winners, Emmy winners, champions, business owners, and a fighter pilot, among others.

The second section of the book, titled Talk, turns the attention from children to fathers, offering advice, strategies, tips, and tactics that you can use to improve everything from work/life balance to your marriage, to handling serious health challenges or even more difficult, health problems with your children. The Talk segment combines actionable advice with stories and plenty of lessons learned from fathers who have built *Fortune* 500 companies, started brewing empires, served in the Navy, founded major fitness brands and accomplished much more as fathers and men.

The last third of the book, which we call Talents, is dedicated to activities and skills you and your kids can do (and get better at) together. It will offer you expert advice on all kinds of real-world hobbies you can do with your kids; from grilling to guitar, to juggling, to improving your basketball shot, to getting stronger and healthier, the legendary fathers we interviewed here have your back.

While you could read this book from front to back, we highly encourage you to jump around to whatever sections or interviews are most relevant to you right now. We're aware that not every chapter is for every dad, but we're confident that every dad can learn something from almost every chapter.

Now go live your best life of dad,
Jon and Art

Part I
Tools—What to Teach

Talk to enough dads about their hopes and dreams for their children and many of them will start out with specifics and then eventually default to something along the lines of "I just want them to be good people. I want them to be happy and healthy. That's really it."

Easier said than done.

What makes a good person? What makes a person happy? Yes, we have a few generally accepted traits that we ascribe to "good" people, and we know of several "needs" that can be met that typically lead to happiness, but even if you somehow figure out concrete answers to those two questions, how do you raise another human being to achieve them?

The best we can do is pass along to our children the traits and values we believe make up a good person. The most we can hope for is that we instill in our kids the mentality and the confidence and resources to go after the things that make them happy. That is what Part I of this book is about: how to teach your kids about positive mindset, character, work ethic, humility, values, and wisdom.

What follows is world-class dad advice from NFL Hall of Famers, Grammy winners, Emmy winners, champions, business owners, a fighter pilot, entrepreneurs, comedians, musicians, and so many more fathers who have the same goal as you: to raise good kids who are happy, healthy, and humble.

CHAPTER 1

Mindset

"Whether you think you can or you think you can't, you're right."
—Henry Ford, Father of One

The Importance of a Positive Mindset
John Elway

DADOGRAPHY

Twitter: @JohnElway
Born: June 28, 1960
Kids: Jessica, Jack, Juliana, Jordan
Career: NFL Hall of Famer, Two-Time Super Bowl Champion, NFL Executive

For the first seven years of John Elway's NFL career, he was pro football's Sisyphus—three times leading his team to the Super Bowl only to lose each game and have to start all over the next season. It would have been understandable if negative thoughts and a defeatist mindset dragged him down after that third loss: "You're too old." "You'll never get to a fourth Super Bowl." "You're past your prime."

But Elway believed in his teammates. He believed in his coaches. And most of all, he believed in himself. Rather than retire, Elway closed out his career with back-to-back Super Bowl wins in 1997 and 1998, capping things off by earning the game's MVP award at age thirty-eight. (He has since added a ring as the team's general manager and vice president after he famously lured Peyton Manning to Denver.)

His belief in the power of positive thinking has crossed over directly from the pigskin to his parenting philosophy. When discussing what he is most proud of in his four children he points to the importance of being kind to other people and, of course, that all-powerful "P" word again—positivity.

LOD: As a father, what is the best advice you have ever given your children?

JE: Well, I'm blessed with four beautiful kids. I think the best advice that I have tried to give to them is something that was passed down to me from my mother and father. It is to treat others the way you would want to be treated. I think if you go through life with that mindset, you will have a lot of good things happen to you. I believe in luck, but I also believe in a positive mindset. If you have that, good things will happen. My kids are hard workers, and I am very proud of them. They do have that positive mindset that good things will happen to them.

The Takeaway: Instill a Mile-High Mindset

Most of us don't have the option of turning on NFL Films to show our children the moments in our lives when we overcame obstacles and negativity and hard times to achieve positive results (or win championships!). Still, that doesn't mean we shouldn't act as if a camera isn't always on us during moments of adversity—because, in essence, it is.

Sure, Elway can show his kids clips of "The Drive," but if you think about it, we all have opportunities to talk about the power of positive thinking with our children too. Whether they're having trouble learning a golf grip, struggling with guitar lessons, or stuck on a geometry problem, we can take a minute to help our kids believe in themselves. When they succeed, they'll keep that lesson with them forever.

We Must Instill Confidence in Our Kids
Chris Jericho

DADOGRAPHY

Twitter: @IAmJericho
Born: November 9, 1970
Kids: Ash, Sierra (SiSi), Cheyenne
Career: WWE Superstar, Author, Actor, Musician, Podcaster

For the sake of this chapter, let's stipulate that somewhere between 40 percent and 60 percent of preteens and teenagers, at some point in their childhood, think it would be awesome to grow up to be a rock star or a WWE wrestler or a *New York Times* bestselling author or a hit podcaster...or any combination of these things. Let's also stipulate that roughly 99.9 percent of the tens of millions of kids who have these dreams will be told that achieving just one of them is largely impossible, let alone racking up several.

These aforementioned teenagers will tell an adult that they want to write the defining novel of their time or have the most downloaded podcast or appear on *Monday Night Raw*, and some beaten-down old person will roll his eyes and say "no," which Chris Jericho, a man who dreamed those same dreams and made them happen, says is a four-letter word.

All it takes is to read one of Jericho's *New York Times* bestselling books (he has three) or to listen to one of his hit podcasts (he's recorded over 450 of them) or to watch him strut out of an arena's tunnel to his famous "Break the Walls" entrance music (he's done this thousands of times) to know that he is not a man who lets others tell him what to do. And don't you dare tell his kids (he has three of those too)—or your own kids—that they can't do something.

LOD: You have so many great themes in your books and podcasts that people should adopt. What is one big one you hope to instill in your kids?

CJ: Confidence. If you want to do something, then make it happen. That said, if you are 5'5" and you want to be the center for the L.A. Lakers, that is not going to happen. You can do whatever you want in life within the limits of the talents that you have and the attitude that you have and the skill level that you have.

The most important thing that you need to have is the confidence and courage to just try. Do things. Don't worry about failure. Don't worry about doing things the wrong way. "No" is a four-letter word. It is an evil word that is accepted far too easily. Instead of accepting the word "no," just figure out how you can make that "no" a "yes."

The Takeaway: Adopt a "No Is a Four-Letter Word" Mentality

One of the best things about talking to Jericho is that because he has accomplished so much, it is very difficult to ignore any of his advice. After all, the man has filled everything from stadiums to cruise ships with his charisma and talent. When we talk to our kids about their careers and their goals, far too often our own practical side wants to leap out and nip what we deem to be a "crazy idea" or a "ridiculous goal" in the bud. It's obviously in our nature to steer our kids toward the best chances of happiness and success, and that's understandable. But the next time this moment presents itself, and your son or daughter wraps up their pitch, before you use the "four-letter word" and immediately put the brakes on what seems like an impractical idea, why not indulge it for a bit?

Talk it out.

Have an open conversation with your kids exploring all the reasons this crazy dream *could* work and see where that gets the both of you. Or, as Jericho might say, "Slap yourself in the face. Get out there and make it happen."

It's Okay to Try to Be Number One
Alfonso Ribeiro

DADOGRAPHY

Twitter: @Alfonso_Ribeiro
Born: September 21, 1971
Kids: Sienna, Alfonso Lincoln Ribeiro Jr., Anders
Career: Actor, Writer, Host

You either know Alfonso Ribeiro from the hit TV shows he's appeared on or the dance. The dance, aka "the Carlton," is a little arms-swinging, finger-snapping, hip-wagging set of moves that Ribeiro performed while playing Will Smith's cousin, Carlton Banks, on the iconic TV show *The Fresh Prince of Bel-Air*. Even though the last episode appeared twenty-two years ago, the Carlton has enjoyed a second life now as one of the most popular social media GIFs of all time.

This is fitting, since before starring on *Fresh Prince* and his other hit show as a child actor, *Silver Spoons,* Ribeiro played the lead role in a dance-heavy Broadway musical and famously appeared in a Pepsi ad with Michael Jackson. A powerful part of examining Ribeiro's storied Hollywood career is seeing just how hard he worked to earn the roles he made famous.

While talking to Ribeiro about his career and his life as a father of three children, he's adamant about passing on the hard lessons he learned in the entertainment business to his family. In fact, he unapologetically swims against the "everyone wins/participation trophy" tide that often has a foothold in kids' sports and activities. He believes in trying to win, fostering a successful attitude, and above all, daring to be great.

LOD: You've survived and thrived in the entertainment industry since you were a kid. What is the main core value that you'd like to pass along to your kids so they can have success in whatever field they choose?

AR: I say this all the time—and crazily enough, I get in trouble for it with some people—but my number one core value is that I have always viewed second place as the first loser. In my business, that is true. One person gets the job. There is no, "Oh, we are going to hire three people. They are all going to do the job. When it is all done, we will pick one." It doesn't work that way. They pick one person to do the job. That's who gets it and the others didn't. It didn't matter if you were second or one hundredth—you still lost. The drive to be great has always driven me in everything that I do. I understand you are not going to win everything. I understand that you very rarely win…but if you are not trying to be the best, then you are not giving it your all. That is something that I feel is really important.

The Takeaway: Support the Drive to Be Great

Ribeiro's actions and words provide a strong counterpoint to the "participation trophy" mindset many parents are hesitant about celebrating. The concern is that rewarding kids for participating with a ribbon or trophy gives them the idea that "everyone is a winner" and success isn't earned. Yet, whether we're talking about Hollywood, business, medical school, or almost every career, quite often there is only one person who gets the job or one test students must pass to earn a degree. There's no reward for participating in real life—and many parents want to teach kids that lesson earlier rather than later. Participation trophies can give kids the incorrect notion that they don't have to earn success. Yet just like Hollywood roles, any career your kids go into is going to be unforgiving, so it's better to prepare them for the hard work ahead of them.

Later in our interview, Ribeiro says that when talking to his kids about winning and losing, he has no problem praising their efforts and being proud of them and telling them they did a good job; he simply won't tell them they "won" if they didn't. He wants them to know that it's okay to want to be number one…and that it's also okay not to be first. But striving for first place and giving everything you have to win first place is the most important. "You have to accept loss," he says. "But you have to strive and do everything you can to be the best that you can be."

We agree.

Prioritize Happiness
Mike Greenberg

DADOGRAPHY

Twitter: @ESPNGreeny
Born: August 6, 1967
Kids: Nicole, Stephen
Career: Sportscaster, Journalist, Author

For nearly two decades, millions of people woke up and listened to Mike Greenberg talk sports. He was one-half of ESPN's flagship morning radio show, *Mike & Mike in the Morning*, along with Mike Golic. Greenberg, aka "Greeny," has said that being paired with Golic was the most important thing to happen to him in his career. But at first, the show wasn't a hit. Nor was it even something Greenberg wanted to do. In fact, he had next to no interest in hosting a morning radio show when he was offered the job. There were a myriad of reasons, chief among them the 3 a.m. alarm clock he'd have to set every day to host a show starting at 6 a.m. Also, he was a TV guy—what was he going to do on the radio?

He accepted the gig as a short-term stepping stone to get where he really wanted to go, which was behind ESPN's signature *SportsCenter* desk. Then a funny thing happened. Despite the eyelid-peeling wake-up time, he enjoyed going to work. Despite not really knowing Mike Golic, they had chemistry. And despite not wanting the job, he enjoyed it. Almost twenty years later, "Greeny" and Golic were inducted into the National Radio Hall of Fame. The lesson he learned: stick with what makes you happy.

When we interviewed Greenberg, he made a point of telling several stories to us about the importance of prioritizing happiness in his life and how he's teaching his son and daughter to make it a priority in theirs.

LOD: You've accomplished so much in your field. What is the most important value you've relied on that you want to pass along to your kids?

MG: When it comes to my kids, I believe happiness is a goal unto itself. My favorite quote that I ever read—and I don't know how fully accurate it is or not—is about John Lennon. When he was five years old, he was asked in school what he wanted to be when he grew up. He said he wanted to be happy. The teacher said, "You don't understand the question." John Lennon said, "No, I don't think you understand life."

Now, that is probably not a fully accurate story. I think we have gotten too hung up on what colleges our kids are going to go to. My kids are right in the height of that conversation. What success that they are going to have professionally and all of that.

I think happiness comes in a lot of different forms. I always tell my kids whatever you want to do in your life, if it makes you happy, it is good with me. I know people who make a lot of money who are absolutely miserable in their lives. They wake up every morning miserable to go to work. At least for me, that would not be a worthwhile trade-off.

The Takeaway: Being Happy Is a Goal Unto Itself

Greenberg's quote about "happiness being a goal unto itself" has always stuck with us because you don't hear "happiness" being described that way too often. Most goals we set for our kids involve concrete achievements, like getting certain grades or making a team or progressing with an instrument or finishing specific books. What if we set the goal for our kids as "happiness" and work backward from there? Won't we then find the things they enjoy and encourage them to pursue those things? Won't they then have more passion for those things and be more successful at them? Seems to us, that's the whole point of life.

Using Experience As a Teaching Tool
Jermaine Dupri

DADOGRAPHY

Twitter: @JermaineDupri
Born: September 23, 1972
Kid: Shaniah
Career: Rapper, Music Producer, Record Executive, Actor, DJ, TV Producer

Uber producer/rapper/actor/writer (and a whole bunch of other entertainment slashes) Jermaine Dupri has never had confidence issues about any of the roles he's had in his life…except for one: dad. Yes, the man who has worked with everyone from Mariah Carey and Usher to Kris Kross and Lil Wayne, and whose classic rap "Money Ain't a Thang" featuring Jay-Z still gets airplay twenty years after it came out, told *Life of Dad* that when he found out he was going to be a father, he was "scared, nervous, and afraid." Welcome to the club, Mr. Dupri.

Dupri was raised in Atlanta, and as he was coming up in the music business, he took great care to let people know that the ATL was his city. He tried to attend every festival, event, and concert to stay involved in the fabric of the city's music scene and ride the tide as it went national. As he got older, it occurred to him that by staying in Atlanta, he missed out on a lot of experiences, from going to college to exploring new cities. Once he had his daughter, he was concerned that his lack of experience would hold his daughter back, so he has pushed her to do more, see more, and live more in her younger years than he ever did. In a way, learning and exploring has become one of his parenting mantras.

LOD: What are some of the core values that you've hoped to instill in your daughter?

JD: Just to learn and explore. I am pushing my daughter, Shaniah, to learn and explore and see more than I did. I have seen a lot, but there was so much more that I could have seen. I was really focused on one thing. That one thing was making sure my roots were as strong as they possibly could be here in Atlanta. I wanted to stay here at all times and make sure that I went to parties. Made sure that I was the one people saw all the time.

As I got older, I realized that I missed out on a lot that I could have seen. A lot of people I idolized or who were like mentors to me, like Quincy Jones, stayed in different cities and got opportunities to see what life is like in different places. I think that helps you become a much more well-rounded person. You can adapt to these different places.

My daughter is about to go to college in Miami. She said that she wanted to go to Miami from the beginning. I think she put that out into the universe and it came back. That is where she is going. I am happy she is going because she will be a more well-rounded person than me. She is going to college. I didn't go to college. She is living in a different city. My daughter will live in a different city before she is twenty-one years old, and I didn't do that. That is a whole life experience that I have never had. So that alone makes me excited.

The Takeaway: Experience Is a Thang

What's most interesting about Dupri's emphasis on his daughter having more experiences than he did is that it's not as if his decisions led to failure. The path he chose led him to tremendous success professionally; however, he felt that by sticking to one thing (music) and one city (Atlanta), he may have shortchanged himself. Somewhere along the line he felt that being a "well-rounded person," as he says, was just as important as the other things in life he valued. Hence, the focus on making sure his daughter was able to do things he didn't, like live in new cities and go to college.

The Power of Standing Up for Yourself
Freddie Prinze Jr.

DADOGRAPHY

Twitter: @RealFPjr
Born: March 8, 1976
Kids: Charlotte, Rocky
Career: Actor, Author

Freddie Prinze Jr. has had two distinct, successful careers in entertainment. In part one, he was the anchor of the *I Know What You Did Last Summer* and Scooby-Doo movie franchises. In part two, he got his own signature lightsaber (it's okay to be jealous, we are too). The saber is for his role as Kanan Jarrus on the hit series *Star Wars Rebels* on Disney XD. While the Scooby-Doo films have enjoyed a major renaissance (at least in the Finkel household) thanks to *Netflix*, it's the lightsaber that has fans of all ages, and Prinze Jr. himself, geeking out. "Star Wars is in my DNA," Prinze Jr. told us. "When I get these monologues and it is talking about the Force and how it is strong in this person, the path to the dark side, and what happened to my Jedi Master, it is huge. For me, it is like a historical reference."

It's fitting, then, that right around the time Prinze Jr. became a father, the fictional Force started flowing through him. Just as Jedi train to battle the dark side and stand up to evil in the galaxy, he was raised to do the same thing, albeit on a more local level, and he's doing his best to pass down that same ethos to his two kids.

LOD: What morals do you want to make sure you pass down to your children?

FP: My uncle James Barber was a Vietnam veteran. He was one of the three main father figures in my life and was certainly the strongest. He believed in standing up for people who couldn't stand up for themselves. I remember when I was in the sixth grade I saw a kid getting beat up by an eighth grader. I didn't do anything because the guy was big.

My uncle taught me how to fight. He was big into martial arts. Instead of learning how to throw spirals I learned the 1-inch punch. So after I saw this kid get beat up, I told my uncle. He got mad at me that I didn't stick up for this kid. He asked me what kind of man I was. I asked him what he meant by that. I get kind of choked up just talking about it. He said, "A real man stands up for people who can't stand up for themselves. If you are any kind of man of mine, you will know that."

The next day at school I went up to the kid and whooped him up so bad. I got sent to the principal's office. My uncle came to pick me up. He acted mad in front of the principal. When we got out of school he patted me on the head and took me to Cliff's, which was an amusement park in Albuquerque, New Mexico. He called me a punk buster. Those are people who see a bully and let them know that they can't do that anymore.

Now, I don't want my kids to be a bully or be bullied. I want them to be self-confident. I want them to know that they can take care of themselves. So those are the main things I try to instill in them. My daughter has been taking jiu-jitsu since she was three years old. She can choke me out already. Martial arts bring a lot of confidence. I hope that I can instill that in my kids. That would be the main thing.

The Takeaway: You Don't Need Your Own Lightsaber to Be Confident

Prinze Jr. is far from the only dad we've talked to over the years who preaches the value of kids taking martial arts. To his point, they offer the dual benefits of teaching confidence and discipline. It's interesting that he juxtaposes his own story of failing to stand up for someone with the importance of his kids being able to protect themselves and perhaps others. As he says, nobody wants their kids to be bullies, but it's equally important that they know how to stand up to one.

Rediscovering Self-Reliance and Grit
Cactus Skidoo

DADOGRAPHY

Twitter: @Agent23Skidoo
Kid: Saki
Career: Musician, Writer, Producer

Billed on his website as the "Grammy-winning, internationally touring, purple velvet tuxedo wearing family funk phenomenon," Secret Agent 23 Skidoo is an artist whose music your three-year-old will remember, your ten-year-old will memorize, and you will find yourself giving props to. Added bonus: his songs aren't just family-friendly; they're actually produced with his family, including his young daughter, Saki, aka MC Fireworks, who legitimately spits bars (raps) with Skidoo on several songs.

As a full-fledged member of the group, Saki has been on tour with her dad for almost ten years and through this unique environment, Skidoo has been able to impart life lessons that many of us can pull into our own, non-global-music-tour parenting lives. Perhaps we won't have the number one song on Sirius XM's family channel, but we can learn a thing or two about what kids are capable of when they're passionate, supported, and understand the gumption it takes to achieve great things.

LOD: What do you hope your daughter learns from growing up in a band and the entire experience surrounding that?

CS: Curiosity and intelligence. Grit. I want my daughter to be challenged. Self-reliance is definitely a big one. We have been talking about what it means to be an honorable hustler. Being a musician, you have to be a hustler. You've got to see the angles that don't exist yet. See angles that no one else is looking for. Since I have come up in the hip-hop world and have a hip-hop mentality, I think of that as hustling.

We talk about honor all the time. That is a really big thing in my household. I don't believe in politeness. I don't believe in manners. I believe in honor, and I believe in respect. Manners and politeness are based on a series of rules that are essentially arbitrary. Honor and respect is an amiable tendency where you have to look into the heart and soul of the people that you are dealing with and figure them out.

I promote honor hardcore. I said to her since we talk about honor a lot, what does it mean if you combine honor and a hustler? What is in the middle? To try and get out of life what you want without exploiting anyone else or anything else and without having a negative impact on anything else. That is what I am trying to promote in her. How can you use all of your intensity, intelligence, curiosity, and love to manifest the life that you want without doing it on the back of anyone else? It is a difficult thought process, but I believe it is possible.

The Takeaway: Hustle & Flow & Honor & Grit

For many of us, singing in the shower or rapping in the car to Maui's "You're Welcome" solo from *Moana* is as close as we'll come to a music career, so the possibility of raising our kids on the road as part of a successful music act is out of the question. That doesn't mean that we can't learn from Skidoo and teach our kids the positive "hustler" mindset. It was refreshing to hear that Skidoo, who once opened for Run-DMC and Mos Def, has found a way to raise an MC daughter with timeless principles like honor and grit that we can use for our kids who are taking garden-variety piano lessons at school. A middle school recital may be a far cry from a packed arena, but pushing through a hard lesson and respecting your teacher will have the same results.

CHAPTER 2

Character

> "The true test of a man's character is
> what he does when nobody is looking."
> —John Wooden, Father of Two

You Must Teach Accountability
Michael Strahan

DADOGRAPHY

Twitter: @MichaelStrahan
Born: November 21, 1971
Kids: Isabella, Sophia, Tanita, Michael Strahan Jr.
Career: NFL Player, Sports Analyst, TV Host

In nearly every interview about his career (or shall we say, careers), Michael Strahan credits his father for being the most influential and important person in his life. Our discussion was no different. He heaps effusive praise on how his dad raised him, saying, "I was listening and taking advice from someone who I really trusted. I was around him, and I saw the way he lived and the way he walked the walk. Now I hope to do the same thing with my kids."

Despite Strahan walking his own walk along a variety of paths, from Super Bowl champion and NFL Hall of Famer with the New York Giants to TV host on *Good Morning America* to celebrity pitchman and even fashion mogul, the thing he focuses most on is filling the same role for his four kids that his dad filled for him.

Supporter. Confidant. Adviser. All of the above and more. The challenge he has is that his kids have only known him as "Famous Michael Strahan." They were too young (or not born yet) to see all the hard work and tough times that went into Strahan reaching the heights he has. We're glad he was candid with us about those challenges.

LOD: You've set the bar pretty high from a parenting standpoint by wanting to walk in your dad's shoes, a man you've said is the most influential person in your life. What's the most important thing you want your kids to learn that you learned?

MS: Accountability. I think it is about being a good person. Being nice. Working hard. It is about the simple things. I found in my life the simple things have led me to the best things. I don't think life gets too complicated. I think it is as complicated as you make it. I think my kids feel very appreciative of everything because there is always an alternative of somewhere where you don't want to go. That is what helps me with my kids. I tell them that it wasn't always like this [for me].

Also, at the same time, my life is not your life. Don't be banking on daddy to take care of you [laughing]. I had to work and you have to work. A lot of people said that I could have retired [after football]. Yes, I could have retired. I could be sitting in Miami just hanging out. I retired when my twins, who are eleven years old, were three. They don't remember daddy the football player. The older ones remember me as a football player, but still I am their father. How could I retire at thirty-six years old and then tell my kids to work hard?

I did work hard, but they don't remember seeing that. I am giving them an example. That is the most important thing. You've got to be an example to your kids. So I am trying to be a good example to them of how to live your life. How to be nice to people. How to work hard. How to enjoy every day and look on the bright side of things.

The Takeaway: Show, Don't Tell

While most of us aren't in a position to retire at age thirty-six like Strahan, all of us have kids who watch our every move. It is far easier to have your kids learn the value of hard work and accountability by watching you work hard and be accountable. It's the same with how you treat people. It's much easier to let your kids see you be nice than to have to explain to them what being nice is.

For football fans and those into pop culture, Strahan has been in the public eye for almost twenty-five years. It's refreshing to hear that one of his motivations for taking on more projects and capitalizing new opportunities was to show his kids what hard work means. We might not be hosting game shows or designing a fashion line, but whatever it is we do, we can continue to thrive and challenge ourselves so that our children will do the same thing.

Character Is Taught by Example
"Mean" Joe Greene

DADOGRAPHY
Born: September 24, 1946
Kids: Major, Delon, JoQuel
Career: NFL Hall of Famer, Coach

Why are we going to take advice about having character from a man with the nickname "mean"? In real life, he's actually not mean at all (just ask the kid from the Coke commercial). As a college and Pro Football Hall of Famer, four-time Super Bowl champion, and the greatest Pittsburgh Steeler who ever lived, yes, the 6'4", 275-pound defensive lineman was someone who had no problem laying the smack down on the field. Off the field, however, Greene is the father of three kids and spent almost twenty years as a football coach, mentoring younger players—many of whom were missing the same thing from their childhoods that he missed out on: an involved father.

This was not something that Greene took lightly. "When I look back on my life, I can see in retrospect how helpful having a positive male model in my life as a young man would have been," he told us.

With that in mind, Greene took the leadership qualities that made him so successful as a player and transferred them over to his new role as coach, mentor, and father figure. He was determined to show that young men can learn character by following the example of someone displaying character in front of them on a daily basis. In essence, Greene treated his players the same way he treated his three kids.

LOD: What one trait from your football career did you hope to pass down to your children while you raised them?

JG: Oh, that would be character. I was fortunate to be surrounded by so many people who would be described as high-integrity, high-character people. The entire Rooney family, who owns and runs the Steelers, treated me so well....I don't know what kind of career I'd have had without them. And Coach [Chuck] Noll was probably one of the most important men in my life. The way he conducted himself in front of all of us was steady and inspiring. I watched him very closely. I got to Pittsburgh before they ever won anything and I got to see how he reacted when we lost—and when we won our first Super Bowl and when we won our fourth. He was the same man. Honest. Honorable. No BS. I saw that every day for my entire career and I tried to borrow from it as much as I could. Same thing with parenting and coaching: You teach character by showing character.

The Takeaway: Hey Kid, Catch Character

In 1979, Greene starred in one of the most famous Coca-Cola commercials of all time. The premise was that after a tough game, Greene was hurt and wanted to get to the locker room but a kid stops him, tells him he's the greatest, and offers him a Coke. Greene is annoyed, but the Coke makes him feel better and he tosses the kid his jersey, smiles, and the kid says, "Wow, thanks, Mean Joe."

Everyone wins.

It's been forty years since the commercial aired, but as we listened to Greene talk about setting an example and living with character day in and day out, the Coke ad seems just as relevant today. In the ad, nobody was watching and the only person who would have known Greene wasn't nice to the kid was the kid. But if character is defined by what we do when nobody is watching, Greene met the definition there quite nicely—albeit in a commercial. Keep that in mind next time you're alone with one of your own kids. We all work hard and have responsibilities beyond being a parent. Next time you're about to snap or get irritated with your kids because of your own long day or frustrations, think of "Mean" Joe and…be nice.

The Importance of Having a Soft Spot for the Underdog
Steve Byrne

DADOGRAPHY

Twitter: @SteveByrneLive
Born: July 21, 1974
Kids: 2
Career: Actor, Comedian

Comedian Steve Byrne says he's made hundreds of thousands of people laugh over the course of his twenty-year comedy career, but the best laughter he's ever heard is from his kids. Clearly, he's our kind of guy. Byrne began his comedy career in New York City performing as many sets in as many clubs as he could. He even created a documentary called *Thirteen or Bust* about the time he performed thirteen shows in a single night at various clubs throughout Manhattan.

He starred in the TBS sitcom *Sullivan & Son* for three seasons before returning to the stand-up circuit, where he's appeared in numerous specials for Comedy Central.

LOD: Comedians always have a unique outlook on life and people. If you could instill one trait in your children, what would it be?

SB: If I could instill one trait in them, it would be to always have a soft spot for the underdog. I think if you have that, it just does so much more for your life. You can look in the world of comedy and say "that one guy has always had it easy." The truth is, no one has ever had it easy. Everyone in my profession has earned what they got. No matter who you are, you are an underdog. The odds are against you as a comic.

If you view yourself as an underdog; if you view others as an underdog; if you have a soft spot for the underdog…it changes your perspective on life. I think you will develop a softer side for anybody. Instantly, you eliminate the bully factor.

I hope they have that. Your heart almost yearns for the kid that is sitting alone at the lunch table or the person who is alone at a party. You will go over and introduce yourselves to these folks. You do that because you understand what it could be like to be that person. So you go through life with this soft spot for everybody. I think that is the way it should be.

The Takeaway: Being Strong by Having a Soft Spot

There are so many definitions of character, but one that we like involves how you treat people who are going through a difficult time. When it comes to kids, the situations they encounter where they have the chance to show their character are in places like Byrne mentioned: the lunchroom, the playground, a birthday party, etc. If we can raise our kids to be the first to reach out to someone feeling left out or be the first person to sit with the new kid at lunch, then we're doing a great job as parents and as stewards of kindness. And, as Byrne said, we eliminate the bully factor right off the bat.

Hard Work and Character Go Hand-in-Hand
Herman Edwards

DADOGRAPHY

Twitter: @HermEdwards
Born: April 27, 1954
Kids: Marcus, Gabrielle, Vivian
Career: NFL Player, NFL Coach, Analyst, College Football Coach

"You play! To win! The game!" This is the most famous "Herman-ism" from charismatic former NFL player and head coach Herman Edwards, but it's far from the only one. Edwards, who has spent the last several years as an analyst for ESPN and is currently the head football coach at Arizona State University, has built an entire personal brand, including a bestselling book that contains home-spun sayings, inspirational phrases, and allegories about leadership. Because of this, Edwards is a sought-after motivational speaker and many of his best tales involve his father (a World War II veteran) teaching him lessons about character and hard work.

LOD: Your speeches are often focused on leadership, motivation, and positive advice. How do you impart these lessons to your own children?

HE: I would say this: Being a parent is the most powerful form of education. Youngsters need role models more than they need criticism. Too often I think we get caught up in making a living rather than making a difference. I think you have to be a role model and it starts at home. I have said this a lot of times—good character is like good soup. It is made at home. We have to give them hard love. You have to be able to say "no," but you have to explain why you are saying "no." You have to educate your children. Children can't choose their parents. They have no choice.

My father also gave me…a broom. A regular broom, and he gave me chores. He gave me the broom and made me look at it. He asked me what it was, and I said it was a broom. He said it means hard work. He said no matter whatever you accomplish in your life, I hope you become whatever you want to become, but whatever you achieve, don't forget this broom. It is called hard work, and he was right. When I grew up there was no blower. You didn't blow the stuff in someone else's yard. You had to sweep it. Today, as God is my witness, I have a broom and I wear it out. I sweep all the time. It reminds me of my dad. Every time I pick up that broom and sweep I think about my dad.

The Takeaway: You Teach! To Raise! Your Kids!

Which one of the "Hermanisms" Edwards gave in his answer stuck with you the most? Was it "good character is like good soup—it is made at home"? Or was it the broom story? Or was it the phrase about people getting caught up in making a living instead of making a difference?

There is almost too much to unpack from such a short answer, but the idea that character is intertwined with hard work is something many dads should keep in mind. It's almost impossible to have one without the other. How many people of character do you know who are lazy or undisciplined or who don't want to put effort into achieving their goals? Not many. Raise your child to be a hard worker and your chances of them understanding the meaning of having character will certainly increase.

Manners Still Matter
Cam Neely

DADOGRAPHY

Twitter: @CamNeelyFdn
Born: June 6, 1965
Kids: Jack, Ava
Career: NHL Player, NHL Executive

Boston hockey legend Cam Neely led the Bruins in goals in his first full season with the team…and he also racked up over 140 minutes in the penalty box. By the time he was twenty-five years old, he was a beloved icon in Bean Town and had earned the nickname "Bam Bam" Cam for his willingness (and desire) to engage in and end fights on the ice. He was the rare combination of talented scorer and enforcer, which fit the blue-collar mentality of the old Boston Garden faithful. At 6'1", 220 pounds, you couldn't cast a more perfect hometown hero.

While we don't typically associate black-eye–giving hockey brawlers with caring about etiquette and politeness, sans pads and helmet, Neely is a philanthropist who puts a premium on treating people right off the ice. He lost both his parents to cancer in a five-year span in the late 1980s and early 1990s, right at the beginning of what was to be an illustrious career. He immediately started the Cam Neely Foundation for Cancer Care to honor his parents and their dedication to family and integrity. Another way he respects their memory is by making sure both of his kids know the importance of respecting other people.

LOD: What is the number one thing you try to teach your kids in terms of core values?

CN: The big thing my wife Pauline and I try to instill is manners. Saying "please" and "thank you" is very important. If a guest comes to our house, you stand up and introduce yourself. It is really about manners and respecting elders. Treat your siblings and parents the way you want to be treated. That is very important to us. It goes a long way and will stay with them for the rest of their lives. The other thing is education. Our kids are in great schools. I just see the amount of work and what they are learning. I certainly didn't have those opportunities.

The Takeaway: The Hat Trick of Manners

"Please." "Thank you." "You're welcome." These are not difficult things to remember to say, and they are not difficult things to teach your kids to say. But somewhere along the path of rushing to make lunches, getting kids dressed and ready for school, homework, hockey practice, playdates, your job, laundry, errands, and the four thousand other things that take up our time, we slowly let a request without a "please" slip by. Then we let another one slip by. Then our kid gets something, and we don't realize they didn't say "thank you," and that starts to go by the wayside. Same with after someone thanks them for something and they don't even mumble a "you're welcome."

It isn't that we don't think these things are important—far from it. It's just that they're so basic that we let them fall by the wayside as the parenting load gets bigger with more kids and more responsibilities. Sometimes it's good to reset and recalibrate with our kids. It's good to take stock of their foundational behavior and reinforce things like saying "please" and "thank you" and "you're welcome." And if they resist, just tell them you have a friend named Sea Bass from Boston who'll come over and remind them if they don't get in line. Ha.

Consistency of Character Is Crucial
Kurt Warner

DADOGRAPHY

Twitter: @Kurt13Warner
Born: June 22, 1971
Kids: Jesse, Sienna, Kade, Zachery, Jada, Sierra, Elijah
Career: NFL Player, NFL Analyst

There was a period of time following the 1994 NFL Draft (when Kurt Warner was not drafted) and after his tryout with the Green Bay Packers (who cut him) when Warner's job wasn't "quarterback," but shelf stocker at a Hy-Vee grocery store for a salary of $5.50 an hour. Warner knew this was one of those moments in life when you either pick yourself up or let your present circumstances and string of bad luck bring you down. He chose the former.

Rather than obsess about not having a job in the NFL, he signed with the Iowa Barnstormers in the Arena Football League and quickly lit it up. He was a two-time All-Arena League player and used the experience to move one step closer to his dream of being in the NFL with a job as quarterback of the Amsterdam Admirals in the now-defunct NFL Europe. Following that season, he spent 1998 as the third-string quarterback for the NFL's St. Louis Rams (now the Los Angeles Rams). The next year, after an injury to starter Trent Green in the preseason, Warner finally achieved his goal that four years prior seemed impossible: starting NFL quarterback.

What happened next in his career is the stuff of legend: a Super Bowl win, a Super Bowl MVP award, big money contracts, four Pro Bowl selections, and a slew of awards that led him to the ultimate destination: the Pro Football Hall of Fame. After such a meteoric rise, one would be forgiven for letting the fame and money and wins get to your head a bit…but not Kurt Warner. The father of seven walked the walk he now teaches his kids: be humble and maintain a consistency of character when things are going well—and when they're not.

LOD: People often point to your story as one where humility and hard work and perseverance paid off. What traits helped you succeed and which ones are most important to pass along to your kids?

KW: There are so many different things. I think the biggest thing is the consistency of character. I think that is one thing that my career has been built on. Who my wife is has been built on that. It is one thing we want our kids to carry with them regardless of what they do—whether it is in sports or in school or being a friend or amongst siblings, we want them to be consistent with strong character.

I think that is one of the things that we are always trying to instill in our kids. It is about what it means to do the right thing. To stand up for what you believe in. To stand up for other people or stand up for what is right. Those are some of the things that we are always working on. We use our faith, our background, and our history to really drive those messages home.

We believe that if you have good character, you will succeed in life. That will overshadow everything else. We live in a country where unfortunately it doesn't seem to be as important as it used to be. We look too much at skills and making money and all of that stuff as opposed to being men and women of character.

The Takeaway: Maintain a High-Character Mindset, Even When Times Are Low

The phrase "don't let the success go to your head" is often used to caution people from changing who they are once they have achieved the success they've sought for so long. We've all seen far too many athletes (and businesspeople and friends) who haven't heeded that advice and who have completely changed with a big promotion or financial or personal win.

One of the things that most impresses us about Kurt Warner is that from our interview with him, and from what others who have known him a long time say, he is the same exact person today as he was when he was stocking grocery store shelves. No ego. No big-timing. No drama. When talking to our kids about their own success, we can hold up Warner as an example of how to act when the chips are down…and when they're up.

Choose to Be a Force of Character
Chad Hennings

DADOGRAPHY

Twitter: @ChadHennings
Born: October 20, 1965
Kids: Chase, Brenna
Career: NFL Player, Speaker, Entrepreneur, US Air Force Veteran

Brick by brick, three-time Super Bowl champion and fighter pilot Chad Hennings has methodically and purposefully built a life of character. Whether it was his decision to join the US Air Force after high school, or honoring his commitment to serve even after winning the Outland Trophy (awarded to the best college football interior lineman) as a senior with a lucrative NFL career directly ahead of him, or his commitment to fatherhood, or working with his Wingmen Ministry—every choice Hennings makes is heavily weighed and considered with character in mind.

That isn't to say he's perfect… After all, the opening line in his book *Forces of Character* reads, "I stole football cards from a little girl." Of course, he was a kid himself at the time, but part of Hennings's philosophy is to examine our weakest moments in life so as not to repeat them.

After a highly decorated college football career at the US Air Force Academy, Hennings flew forty-five successful combat missions in an A-10 jet during the Gulf War, after which he joined the Dallas Cowboys as a twenty-seven-year-old rookie who hadn't played a down of football in years. As fate would have it, he'd be joining the team at the perfect time, with Troy Aikman, Emmitt Smith, and Michael Irvin about to become offensive legends and his good buddy Charles Haley set to lead the defense to multiple Super Bowls. It was during this hectic and successful time of adjusting to civilian life (albeit, as a Dallas Cowboy) and playing himself into football shape that Hennings also began adjusting to his life's biggest mission: being a dad.

LOD: Where do you think you got this desire to live a high-character life, and how do you pass that desire along to your children?

CH: First and foremost, my identity that I got was from my parents. I grew up on a farm in Iowa. I saw the way that my father worked and the way my grandfather worked. My family's farm has been in my family for over 120 years, and hearing the stories about how they maintained it and worked the land through generations instilled in me the concept of what character is. Knowing I was next in line gave me an identity about how I wanted to conduct myself. My time in the Air Force reinforced those character traits of service and integrity—to be your best self every day.

I have a son and a daughter in college. The one thing that I wanted to get across to them was to take ownership of who they are. Take an identity and be accountable for your actions, your thoughts, your words, and the deeds that you do.

That whole aspect of self-identity is very important to me. Who are you? What does it mean to be a Hennings? This is who we are. This is what we stand for. This is what we try to exemplify in our community. That is important for the legacy that you leave. Every day your thoughts, your words, and your actions matter. I tell my kids that life is a series of choices, so choose wisely.

One phrase that I always share with them is, "he who walks with wise men will be wise." You have to choose your friends and your mentors carefully. In The Prince, *Machiavelli said the best indication of a man's character is the company that he keeps. That is so true. Who are you hanging out with? Who are your friends? That is ultimately what you are going to be defined by.*

The Takeaway: Give Your Kids an Identity to Live Up To

One of the things we loved about this interview is Hennings's focus with his kids on ownership of their identity and the responsibility they have to their family. For Hennings, the family name is important because it represents the traits of integrity and hard work that his father stands for. The name means something.

What do you want your family to stand for? What are the first three traits you want your kids to think about when they think of you? Take some time to ponder these things, and then act according to the identity you aspire to have. Be your own force of character, and then take pleasure in watching your kids become theirs.

The Importance of Being True to Yourself
Kofi Kingston

DADOGRAPHY

Twitter: @TrueKofi
Born: August 14, 1981
Kids: Khi, Orion
Career: WWE Superstar

High-flyin' and smilin' WWE star Kofi Kingston has been a staple of the wrestling universe for more than a decade. He's been a Tag Team Champion, an Intercontinental Champion, and a United States Champion and has done it all with a huge grin on his face—which makes him a rarity (and also a fan favorite) in the WWE. A throwback to the days of Jimmy "Superfly" Snuka, Kingston routinely leaps off turnbuckles, cages, fences, announcing tables, ropes, and almost anything he can climb to soar through the air and take out his opponent. Despite the potential for bodily harm on a nightly basis, Kingston refuses to stop beaming. Why? Because he knows how hard he worked and how far he traveled to get where he is today.

Not only was Kingston born in Ghana, which is 5,000 miles away from the WWE's headquarters in Connecticut, but after graduating from Boston College (where his parents were librarians) he quickly found himself stuck in a cubicle farm like far too many of us. The year was 2005 and Kingston was spending his days proofreading catalogues at Staples's corporate headquarters in Boston. He was bored. He was miserable. He felt deep in his bones that he should be doing something else. Desperately needing to shake things up, he drove down to the Chaotic Wrestling training facility in Tewksbury, Massachusetts, and the moment he stepped inside, he knew his life was about to change for the first time. He'd become a WWE star a few short years later.

The second time his life changed was when he became a father. "You have a sense of pride just to be a father and a parent," he told us. "To have somebody depend on you so much and be able to deliver is awesome. It is the best."

LOD: You perform for thousands of people every week on *WWE SmackDown*, and you preach positivity to your fans. What other traits do you work on with your own kids?

KK: I want my kids to stay true to themselves. There were a lot of times when I was growing up that I wanted to either fit in or be like somebody else. Kofi is a very unique name. When I was going to school, I would get made fun of. I would be called "coffee" or other types of names. I was mad at my parents because they didn't name me Joey. I wanted to be called Joey. I was crying. I was asking why they named me Kofi.

Now I take pride in my unique name. I started becoming true to myself. I want to instill that in them at a young age. My oldest—he is three right now—has such a strong personality that he gets from his mom. He definitely knows what he wants. I don't think he is going to have any difficulty in doing his own thing. He does his own thing now. He marches to the beat of his own drum. It is all good.

The Takeaway: Listen to Your Inner Voice

Kingston's finishing move, which is a lightning-fast spinning kick to knock his opponents out, is called Trouble in Paradise. As wrestling fans, we found the kick to be a nice metaphor for the lessons Kingston wants to impart to his kids. When he graduated college, to the outside world, things were going just fine. He had a steady job with a major company and money to pay his bills. To other young men who couldn't find a job after college, he probably appeared to have it all figured out and was on his way to a nice, comfortable life.

Only, Kingston didn't want that life. There was a voice in his head telling him he was meant to do something else and when he followed it, he found true happiness. When it comes to our kids, too often we point them in the direction of "comfortable" and "easy" without taking into account what their inner voices are telling them. Not only is having character about treating other people well, it's about treating yourself well too. Our kids need to know that.

CHAPTER 3

Work Ethic

"If a man is called to be a street sweeper,
he should sweep streets even as Michelangelo painted,
or Beethoven composed music, or Shakespeare wrote poetry.
He should sweep streets so well that all the hosts of heaven and earth will
pause to say, 'Here lived a great street sweeper who did his job well.'"
—Martin Luther King Jr., Father of Four

Dads Must Lead by Example
Shaquille O'Neal

DADOGRAPHY

Twitter: @Shaq
Born: March 6, 1972
Kids: Shareef, Me'arah, Shaqir, Taahirah, Amirah
Career: NBA Player, Analyst, Rapper, Actor, Entrepreneur

Nobody does a better job of introducing Shaquille O'Neal than
Shaquille O'Neal. The four-time NBA champion, cohost of the
Emmy-winning *Inside the NBA* on TNT, and pitchman for
everything from Carnival Cruise Line to Icy Hot has invented a

never-ending list of nicknames for himself to preclude any entrance. Here are some of our favorites: The Diesel, Shaq Fu, The Big Aristotle, The Big Quotatious, The Big Baryshnikov, The Big Shamrock, The Big Shaqtus… And there are about fifty more.

But our number one self-given nickname by Shaq to Shaq is probably no secret: The Big Daddy. Shaq has five children and throughout his career he has always made it clear that they are the top priority in his life. He frequently posts videos from his kids' events on social media, be it a basketball game or high school graduation, talking about the pride he takes in being their dad. And he's made it a point of having them present for his charity events like Shaq-A-Claus, his long-running self-named event (shocking) where he delivers holiday presents and cheer to underprivileged kids.

Yes, the big man has a big heart and a big plate full of responsibilities that he is not afraid to rearrange by trying new things, following his own dreams (be it rapping, acting, DJing, or investing), and leading the way rather than following someone else's path. He's working hard to instill those same traits in his kids.

LOD: With so many careers, interests, and accomplishments to your credit, what are some of the main things you've tried to teach your kids so they reach their own success?

SO: I want to teach them to have fun and to follow their dreams. Of course, their upbringing is a lot smoother than mine. I always tell them that whatever they want to be, they can be. You are always going to have trials and tribulations.

One of my daughters wants to be a singer. I tell her to go do it. If she likes to sing, then go and sing. If she doesn't, well, do something else. It is just like me. When I wanted to start up a certain business, I would go out and do it. If it didn't work, I would go do something else. I try and lead by example.

I try my best to teach my kids to be leaders, not followers. I tell them not to just do something because someone else is doing something. You've

got to know and understand what you are doing. You have to understand
what will happen if you do something.

The Takeaway: Set a Diesel-Sized Example

If you're trying to follow someone's example as a dad, yes, Shaq has
big (literal) shoes to fill. Yet while Shaq may be charting his course
on national TV or attaching himself to major national brands, the
lessons he's imparting to his kids are the same lessons all fathers hope
to pass on to their own kids: be a leader, choose your own path, try
different things, don't be afraid to fail, etc.

Not all of Shaq's moves have worked out. (Have you seen any
of his Mr. Big candy bars from the 1990s around?) The key is that
he's always explored new opportunities and put himself out there.
You can do the same…without worrying about your kids Googling
Kazaam and wondering what you were thinking when you took that
role. Ha! Just kidding, Shaq. We're *Kazaam* fans.

There's No Substitute for Hard Work
J.B. Smoove

DADOGRAPHY

Twitter: @OhSnapJBSmoove
Born: December 16, 1965
Kid: Jerrica
Career: Actor, Writer, Comedian, Director

As an up-and-coming comedian, J.B. Smoove hated his day job, but
he needed it to keep the lights on. He'd work all day and then perform at clubs all night while trying to hit some college stand-up gigs

and events on the weekends. It was tiresome and wearing him out, but he couldn't survive on the side money he made from comedy alone. Plus, he had a daughter on the way. The sensible thing to do would have been to give up the comedy career and focus on the day job, or at the very least, keep grinding in both until he got a career break in entertainment.

Smoove chose neither path.

Instead, he did what many would consider unthinkable. He quit his nine-to-five job on the day his daughter was born. Even talking about it now he recognized how insane that decision was, but as he says, "I believe that you've got to release something for you to allow something new to come through. Me releasing that job on that day was crazy."

But then, he found that he was completely reinvigorated. With no safety net and no more excuses about not being able to audition or have time for TV roles or movie roles or to sit down and write, he put his nose to the comedy circuit grindstone and got to work. Hard.

LOD: Your entertainment career in many ways is the definition of determination and perseverance paying off. What are other values you look to instill in your daughter?

JS: Work hard. I think that alone is a huge thing. She knows about that. We have talked about that. My daughter has changed her major twice. She sees the hard work that I put into my career, and that in itself shows her how to work hard. My daughter is a student. She has her own pie company. She also worked for Habitat for Humanity. These are a nice range of things for her to get inspired by.

All of these things she was doing at the same time while she was in college. That shows a whole wide range of different levels of the influence I have had on her: Go after what you want to in life. Enjoy your ride. She has a wonderful sense of humor. She has a wonderful outlook on what life is. She is a free spirit. My daughter is basically a hippie (laughing).

She is grounded too. She knows that she has to work hard to get everything that she wants. Her grade point average was amazing in college. She has the ability to expand on that. These are all things that you have to instill into your kids to allow them to flourish and grow. I can't wait for the next wave of what she is going to do.

The Takeaway: Things Won't Always Go Smoove-ly

Has anyone reading this willingly quit their job on the day their first kid was born? Barring a health issue, can you think of anything gutsier and potentially more disastrous? It takes a special kind of confidence and work ethic to believe in yourself enough to pick that time to make that move. Clearly, retelling that story to his own daughter has instilled an entrepreneurial spirit in her, and we could tell from talking to Smoove how proud of his daughter he is and how much she now inspires him.

When talking to older kids about work ethic (and comedy), show them old episodes of *Curb Your Enthusiasm* to learn from Smoove's character, Leon, about how not to be the ultimate freeloader... And then tell them the real story about Smoove so they can learn about being the ultimate free thinker. When that conversation's over, you can do some lampin' together.

Teach Children to Earn Everything
Mike Golic

DADOGRAPHY

Twitter: @ESPNGolic
Born: December 12, 1962
Kids: Mike Jr., Jake, Sydney
Career: NFL Player, Sports Broadcaster, Author

The Golics are first and foremost a football family. Mike Golic's dad, Bob Golic Sr., played in the Canadian Football League and won a Grey Cup (that league's Super Bowl). All three of Bob Golic Sr.'s boys, Greg, Bob, and Mike, played football at Notre Dame. Bob Jr. became an All-Pro in the NFL, and Mike had an eight-year NFL career. Then Mike's sons, Jake and Mike Jr., played football at Notre Dame (his daughter swam there) and both flirted with NFL careers.

DNA, inherent athletic ability, and size were certainly determining factors when it comes to the Golic family's gridiron and swimming achievements, but Mike Golic, who has gone on to even bigger success after football with his Hall of Fame radio career and ESPN studio jobs, says there is an even stronger factor in all three of his kids' athletic and life success: work ethic.

LOD: You come from a family of athletes and have raised a family of athletes. What traits or values have you instilled in your kids that have allowed them to achieve their own success?

MG: It was the same core values that I grew up with and my wife grew up with. If you want to get somewhere in life, it is going to take hard work. There is no shortcut to success at all. We were really old school in my upbringing. My wife was as well with her parents.

We had the same values with our kids. Our philosophy when we were starting to have kids was that we were going to support our kids 100 percent. We will support anything that they do. Get behind them any way we can. We will teach them the value of hard work. Obviously, education is important, but hard work is important for anything that you want to achieve, especially in an era where we have a microwave society. Everything can be done kind of quick, and there are shortcuts that people want to take in life. We teach them that you can't really do that to find success. There can never be a shortage of hard work at all. We really, really tried to instill that value into our kids.

The Takeaway: There Are No Shortcuts

What Golic calls a "microwave society" we like to call a "touch-of-the-button" society. In the world our kids are growing up in, nearly every thing they need—from books to concert tickets, video games, new phones, new sneakers, fast food, and even a fresh mattress—can all be selected, ordered, and then delivered following the touch of a button on their smartphone. And even that concept is dated. With Alexa and Siri and "Ask *Google*," our kids can now order things just by talking to their devices.

With that much convenience at our kids' fingertips, it is more important than ever to teach them that while ordering "things" is easy, the "things" needed to be successful in life are the same as they have always been: hard work, persistence, integrity, perseverance. Golic says those things are old school, and in many ways they are, but in this case, old school is the only school that matters. Let your kids see you getting up early to exercise. Show them how you prepare for your day. Let them see you start and finish a project. Those lessons will resonate louder than any lip service about hard work.

The Key to Having No Regrets
David Otunga

DADOGRAPHY

Twitter: @DavidOtunga
Born: April 7, 1980
Kid: David Jr.
Career: WWE Superstar, Lawyer, Actor

In our current business climate of side hustles, dual jobs, and second careers, few people can match David Otunga's hyphenate of WWE superstar–professional lawyer. He is the rare (and only) individual to walk this earth with both Harvard Law School graduate and WWE Tag Team Champion on his curriculum vitae. And he wouldn't have it any other way.

Flashback to a twenty-six-year-old Otunga, fresh out of law school and having just passed the bar, working at the prestigious Sidley Austin LLP law firm, making great money, living in a fancy place with an absurdly bright future ahead…and yet, something was gnawing at him. It started out as a low hum in his bones and it gradually grew to a heavy bass echoing through his subconscious: *You were meant for more than this. You know what you want. Don't ignore your dreams. Now is the time!*

Rather than continue to stifle this feeling, he let it free, quit the firm, and went after his goal of becoming an actor and WWE star, knowing one day his story would be the example that his son David Jr. would follow.

LOD: You've had one of the most unique careers we've come across, and it's an excellent lesson for kids about not living with regret. How did you make it happen?

DO: Ever since I was a kid, I always had really big dreams. I knew that I wanted to be in the WWE. I wanted to be an actor. I grew up looking up to guys like Hulk Hogan, who just came back to the WWE. I grew up idolizing Hulk. I was a big Hulkamaniac. I like guys like Arnold Schwarzenegger and Sylvester Stallone. Guys who were muscular and had great physiques is what drove me into bodybuilding. I always knew that it was something that I wanted to do, but my mom told me that I needed to have a fallback career, which is actually great advice.

I was always trying to make it into entertainment, but nothing was really sticking. All the way, I was still going to school and getting good grades. I eventually earned a degree and landed a job at a top law firm in Chicago. I was enjoying it. It was a great firm, but I still wanted to follow my dreams. Ultimately I had to make a huge decision. If I stay at the firm, I would probably be happy, but I would always regret not going after my dream and seeing what I could do. I made the decision to leave the firm and go after it. Fortunately, I made it. I was able to accomplish my dream. I am glad I decided to do that. It turned out to be a great decision.

The Takeaway: How Do You Like Them Apples?

It's very difficult for young kids to understand what regret is. Sure, they can comprehend making a decision that they ultimately shouldn't have made and that they may feel badly about, but the idea of "living with regret" can only be learned by staring a decision directly in the face, choosing a path, and sticking with it…only to feel years or decades later that it was the wrong choice.

The flip side to that coin is choosing to do nothing when a new opportunity or idea presents itself. Quite often, the idea of having regret is just as likely to come from the road not taken as the road taken. As dads, we draw upon our own life stories to teach our kids lessons about all kinds of things…regret being one of them.

Otunga's story is important for his own son and for other dads to hear because he embodies the idea of not living with regret. At twenty-six years old, he could have easily stuck with his law career and probably had a great life… But then we wouldn't be writing about him—and he'd be telling his son about the time he *should have* left his law firm to try and become a wrestler and he's always regretted not doing it…rather than the story about how he *did leave* and it was the best career decision he ever made.

On Overcoming Procrastination
Chris Cole

DADOGRAPHY

Twitter: @ChrisCobraCole
Born: March 10, 1982
Kids: Wyatt, Penelope
Career: Skateboarder, Entrepreneur

"Live rad and die proud" is more than just a saying for street skater Chris Cole—it is his guiding principle in life. At the age of fourteen, Cole was lucky enough to find his life's calling, skateboarding. As a young teenager living just outside of Philadelphia, Cole entered as many local and regional skateboarding contests as he could, and he quickly discovered something pleasant: not only did he love skateboarding—he was amazing at it.

As he won more and more contests, Cole's name spread throughout the skateboarding industry and as he garnered fans, trophies, and praise, corporations took notice. By age sixteen, Cole earned his first corporate sponsorship, which helped to launch his professional career. He was named *Thrasher* magazine's "Skater of the Year" twice and won back-to-back street skate gold medals at the X Games.

Now, at thirty-seven years old and with two kids of his own, he's showing them how to give back through his skate camp, Chris Cole's Excellent Adventure, through his work with the Police Athletic League in Philadelphia, and by showing them how to build upon success by following his own entrepreneurial spirit and avoiding what used to hold him back.

LOD: What is the best advice that you've received that you now pass on to your kids?

CC: Every single day when I drop off my son at school I tell him to study hard and learn a lot. That was what my mom told me every day when she would drop me off at school. We are really candid with our kids. We show them that we are human and that we make mistakes.

Some of the mistakes that I have made are procrastinating and putting off work. When I was in school, all I wanted to do was skateboard. I tell my son that and how I really didn't pay attention. I would sit and suffer through the fact that I didn't do my homework. I would just suffer for hours thinking about it. I had anxiety because I didn't do the homework and be in fear all day long. I would freak out about it for hours instead of just spending the twenty minutes it would take me to get it done. I really tried to get that through to him. Don't put it off. Don't make it this monster. Just do it and you will be so much happier.

The Takeaway: Kickflip over Procrastination

Chris Cole participates in several charities, has owned and invested in several businesses, has aligned himself with a myriad of brands for sponsorships and partnerships, owns his own skate park, and also, you know, is a professional athlete. Knowing all that, it seems like procrastination and putting things off wouldn't exactly be in his DNA, but after talking to Cole, we appreciated how down to earth he is and how honest he is about his own shortcomings and things that held him back as a kid.

Maybe procrastinating isn't something that you struggled with. Or maybe you're exactly like Cole. Either way, letting your kids know that even the most successful people can struggle with anxiety and putting things off is important so they don't think they're the only ones. His advice to "don't make [projects/homework/whatever] this monster" is spot on. That's something we're all guilty of at some point.

On Kids Following in Your Footsteps
Steven Curtis Chapman

DADOGRAPHY

Twitter: @StevenCurtis
Born: November 21, 1962
Kids: 6
Career: Musician, Grammy Winner

With nearly a half-dozen Grammy Awards, forty-eight career number one radio singles, and eleven million records sold, Steven Curtis Chapman is a bona fide Christian music icon. He has been featured on *The Tonight Show*, CNN, *Good Morning America*, *Fox & Friends*, and *Today*, among countless nationwide tours to sold-out stadiums.

He is also the author of the book *Between Heaven and the Real World: My Story*, which chronicles his life, from childhood to his marriage to his life as a father, which included touring and performing with his sons, Caleb and Will, for several years. Talking about that time in his life illustrates Chapman's thoughts on how he has tried to guide his children while also building a powerful bond with them.

LOD: While your book is an honest and open look at your whole life, what ideas about fatherhood do you hope men take away from it, especially in the area of kids choosing similar careers as their parents?

SCC: I hope I lived a life of advice and encouragement. The really beautiful thing is that if my sons chose careers in finance, I would have been a terrible advice giver. Hopefully not because I have been foolish financially. That is just not my world. Had they chosen an athletic career, they knew when they were seven years old that they were schooling dad out on the basketball court. [He laughs.] They were like, "Dad is going to be zero help to us there."

It was certainly not by my design that they chose music. My wife and I tried to discourage it. We were like, "You don't want a career in music." You don't want to go that direction. Get a real job. My dad told me the same thing. I was a pre-med major for about fifteen minutes. I saw the light and knew it wasn't going to work. They just began early on to show these great gifts for music. Thankfully, I got to apprentice them in a way. They went on tour with me for about five years. They started playing in my band because they were just that good.

I had this amazing four- to five-year journey where I got to have them on tour with me. Just spending time with two guys who are my best friends. They are two people that I love hanging out with who happen to be my sons. They would watch and observe how I did things. They will come and ask, but they are going in a different direction with their music. They are doing things that I have never done. They are doing it on their own terms. There are many places they go where people don't know who I am or that they are related to me. They ask me advice on things.

It has been an incredible blessing. What a gift. To get to watch my sons get to do something that they are passionate about. It is such a cool thing.

The Takeaway: Advise, Encourage, and Support

We all have dreams for our children that may include our own passions, but it's extremely important that we let our children find their own path. If their own path turns out to be similar to yours, take advantage of that situation and offer any advice and encouragement you can based on your experience. Maybe you can help your kid avoid a mistake you made or learn something about the industry they might not otherwise know. In Chapman's case, who knows what would have happened if Chapman had forced a musical career on them? They might have never discovered their own passion for it and maybe they'd be giving terrible financial advice somewhere. Ha!

Finding Inspiration from Your Kids
Jeffrey Brown

DADOGRAPHY

Twitter: @jeffreybrownrq
Born: July 1975
Kids: 2
Career: Cartoonist, Author

We all have our own favorite Star Wars movie, and we all have our own opinions on the spin-offs and reboots and pre-trilogies and post-trilogies and storylines, but one thing we should all be able to agree on is that as far as kids' books that tie in the Stars Wars universe go, Jeffrey Brown's acclaimed *Darth Vader and Son* book is the best. There have been four follow-ups so far and all have landed on *The New York Times* Best Seller list. The first book won the prestigious Eisner Award, which is given for creative achievements in comic books.

One of Brown's other popular books, *Kids Are Weird: And Other Observations from Parenthood,* was directly inspired by real situations with his two sons. In fact, he used direct quotes from one of his sons in the book and made sure that while he was writing it, he checked with him for accuracy. Far more than just using his kids as inspiration for his work, he has embraced the process and thinks of it more as a collaboration in many ways.

LOD: How much of your books come from real-life scenarios with your kids, and what is it like to "work" with them on a project you're writing and drawing?

JB: Even when I first started writing comics, my art has always been inspired by observing the everyday, little moments. Even the Star Wars books draw on my own experiences and observations. Kids Are Weird *is a tribute to my son. It shows how smart and funny kids can be without even realizing it. I was just trying to capture that in the comics form. Because* Kids Are Weird *is all things that he had actually said, I wanted to make sure it stayed true to life. We went through all the ideas before I drew them out. I double-checked with him to make sure he was okay with everything I put into the book. He calls it his happy book.*

The Takeaway: Capture Moments Creatively

One of the best ways for teenagers and young adults to understand what your relationship was like when they were little is for them to read your own words about it. Brown is able to do this through his books, but we can do it another way. Rather than only snapping a million pictures on your phone for every occasion, try writing down your thoughts on the experience in a journal or a notebook on your phone or computer. If possible, have your kids do the same thing. Capturing that moment in time, what you were both feeling from different perspectives, and then looking at what you wrote together later in life can provide some funny perspective on what you and your kids remember.

The Pride of Overcoming Challenges
Jamaal Charles

DADOGRAPHY

Twitter: @JCharles25
Born: December 27, 1986
Kids: Makenzie, Makaila
Career: NFL Player

When National Football League fans, college football fans, and fantasy football fans think of Jamaal Charles, they usually think of one word: stud. Charles is a four-time NFL Pro Bowler, BCS National Champion (with the University of Texas), and one of the most dynamic rushers in all of football from 2010 to 2015. He currently holds the record for most average yards per carry by a running back with 5.4 yards.

What fans don't think of (likely because they don't know) is what Charles overcame to achieve his success. Despite being born a gifted athlete, he was also born with a learning difficulty that went undiagnosed for so long that he was able to compete in the Special Olympics as a ten-year-old. He was bullied, mocked, and was often the butt of jokes while he was in middle school.

Now that Charles is a father of two young girls, he has chosen to tell the story of how he overcame his childhood obstacles to become the athlete, man, and father that he is today. He partnered with author Sean Jensen on the book *The Middle School Rules of Jamaal Charles*, where he talks about how the gold medals he won at the Special Olympics empowered him and fostered his work ethic, along with his determination to succeed on the field and in the classroom from that point on.

LOD: Your book is about overcoming challenges and not letting other people define you. These are very important lessons for children. What is your main piece of advice when talking to kids who face similar obstacles that you faced?

JC: Just to not get scared when you face a challenge. You can overcome any challenge. Don't get scared just because you have a learning disability. You can overcome those things. I just tell people that you've got to work on the things that you are not strong in. If you just work at the things that you are strong in, then you will never improve in the areas where you are weak. Always stay on the things that you are weak in, because you will become stronger and stronger in those areas.

The Takeaway: Don't Run from Challenges— Tackle Them Head-On

Who better to learn a lesson from about running through barriers in life than a running back? It's far too easy to look at the end results of someone's success and to assume that they had an easy path to get there. This is especially so when it comes to professional athletes, who our kids often put on a pedestal and idolize with posters and bobble heads and replica jerseys.

We've all dealt with the challenge of explaining to our kids that sometimes their favorite athlete isn't such a great person off the field or court. In some cases, getting to know the man under the helmet may not be such a good thing… But in the case of Jamaal Charles, it is.

Ninety-nine percent of fans cheering him on at Arrowhead Stadium in his prime or who drafted him in the first round of their fantasy leagues have no idea the struggles Charles overcame. We commend him for talking about them openly. When other athletes are willing to do the same thing, and they're willing to share the strategies they employed to overcome their difficulties, we should take the opportunity to share those stories with our kids…in addition to sharing the excitement of an 80-yard touchdown run. And let's not forget, your child's biggest inspiration is you! You should absolutely share with them the challenges you've faced in your life and how you overcame them.

The Core Principles of Arthur Blank
Arthur Blank

DADOGRAPHY

Twitter: @BlankFoundation
Born: September 27, 1942
Kids: Danielle, Joshua, Max, Kenny, Kylie, Dena
Career: Home Depot Founder, NFL Owner, Philanthropist

You might not recognize Arthur Blank's name right away, but you've no doubt spent time in his store and watched his team on TV. The store we're referring to is Home Depot, which he cofounded after being fired from another job in 1978 (now there are two thousand

stores), and the team is the NFL's Atlanta Falcons, which he pur-
chased in 2002. Blank, who is equal parts businessman and philanthropist, has had one overriding philosophy throughout his working
life: you can never put your career ahead of your family.

As the head of several successful, large organizations, Blank is
often asked for business and family advice. Over the years, he has
developed certain principles that are applicable in both our professional lives and our lives as parents (Blank would know—he has six
kids!). Our wide-ranging and informative interview with him has
more solid takeaway advice per sentence than any we've done. Enjoy
it and take notes.

**LOD: As the father of six kids, what values from the business
world have you found most important to use in your role as a
parent?**

*AB: Well, to be honest with you, the same values that we build in all
of our businesses that really go back to my days at Home Depot. I was
a cofounder. That value set is not only critical in terms of dealing with
your associates, fans, guests, or whatever the business may be. They are the
same value set that you should have in your home.*

*It is being a good listener. Being able to respond to what you are
hearing both with your family and beyond your family, stand up for
others and give back to your community. It is all of those kinds of things.
Being the best role model that you can be as a parent. I think the greatest
gift that you can give a child is having a home where good examples
are set. Children see that parents have healthy and happy relationships
between the two of them. They can model that behavior in the future. It's
important that regardless of how busy the parents must be in their own
pursuits, the children are not put on the back burner. I think taking care
of family and being there for family is always critical.*

You can't ever put your career in front of your family. Your family is not only your children but your spouse as well....You also can't substitute material things for time with your family.

I think having balance in your life as a father is critical. If I have to give up something, let it be my golf game or tennis match. It is not to say that you shouldn't have time for yourself, because you need to refuel your own tank so you can be there for your own family and work. Your kids and spouse in retrospect are not going to appreciate and understand that the dad is removed from the scene for a certain amount of time even though he is making a lot of money and moving his career along. So I would say find a way to balance your time. Maybe not every day or even every week, but over the course of a month and certainly over a year make sure that your time is balanced between your family and your vocation.

The Takeaway: Great Advice to Take Home from the Home Depot Founder

Arthur Blank was not born as the heir apparent to a *Fortune* 500 company and an NFL team. His dad was a pharmacist and his mom stayed home to raise the children. He worked his way up from the proverbial "humble beginnings," and as he got more successful, he told us he never compromised his set of principles. In fact, the busier he got, the more he relied on them to maintain boundaries between his work life and home life. In our modern society, many men find themselves becoming first-time dads at the precise moment that their careers are beginning to take off. This can cause a lot of anxiety and stress because you're now needed more than ever in two places: work and at home. What you need to do is put together your own list of principles (it's okay to steal some of Blank's) and decide in advance where you will not compromise your family time. Once you have those guiding rules, there are no more "tough" decisions to make.

Treating People Right Is Key
Seth Davis

DADOGRAPHY

Twitter: @SethDavisHoops
Born: 1970
Kids: Zachary, Gabriel, Noah
Career: Sportswriter, Broadcaster, Author

For almost twenty years, Seth Davis was one of the faces of college basketball as a writer for *Sports Illustrated* and a studio analyst for CBS Sports. He's written three books (one *New York Times* bestseller), covered Final Fours, national championship games, and is friendly enough with legendary Duke head basketball coach Mike Krzyzewski that Davis and his kids grabbed photos with Coach K during March Madness. In fact, Davis makes it a point to take his boys to the Final Four every time he can, sharing as much of his career and experiences with them as possible. He takes them to games, into locker rooms to meet players, and even onto CBS's live studio set, where "the camera guys love them and teach them bad words."

Davis is now the managing editor of *The Athletic*'s college basketball site, *The Fieldhouse*, in addition to his in-season TV duties. Despite a seemingly packed schedule, he makes it a priority to work from home, coach his boys' soccer teams, and take them out on the golf course as much as possible.

"I am blessed with what I do," Davis says. "I am not one of these guys that lives to work. I work to live. I have been unbelievably fortunate to be able to manage my life so even though I travel a lot, I have a home office. I am really lucky that I get to be around. I am lucky to be their dad because they are incredible boys."

LOD: It's so great that you have been able to include your kids in your career and prioritize them in your life. What is the number one lesson you look to impart to them with all of this quality time?

SD: It is very simple. It is treat people right. It is easier to say "treat people the way you want to be treated," but I think it should be better than that. Be respectful. I [wrote] a book about John Wooden. He talked about his dad saying, "You are just as good as everyone else, but you are no better than anybody else."

I talk to them a lot about eye contact. When I introduce them to other adults, I say reach out your hand, shake their hand, and look them in the eye and say, "Nice to meet you." Believe me, adults are not used to getting that from seven- and nine-year-old boys. That stuff impresses them. As long as they do a few very important things correctly, I let them do whatever they want. I am not a big strict guy. Certain things I am very, very strict about: manners and respect. Other than that, life is short, have fun, be happy, and enjoy your youth while it lasts, because old guys like you and me know it doesn't last forever.

The Takeaway: Take Your Kids on the Road (Final Four or Not)

Seth Davis has the kind of job that can pull you away from your family on a frequent basis and for long periods of time, but he has chosen to design his life with the opposite purpose: to be around his kids as much as possible. We applaud him on those efforts and encourage all of us dads to think about ways we could maybe include our kids in our lives more. Maybe take them on a business trip if you can? Or to a cool event or office function? Sure, grabbing selfies with Coach K might not be in the cards, but to your little kids, you're the star, and they'll be proud to go anywhere with you.

CHAPTER 4

Values

"We hang on to our values, even if they seem at times tarnished and worn; even if, as a nation and in our own lives, we have betrayed them more often than we care to remember. What else is there to guide us? Those values are our inheritance, what makes us who we are as a people."
—Barack Obama, Father of Two

Embrace the Cheesy Basics
Mark Hamill

DADOGRAPHY

Twitter: @HamillHimself
Born: September 25, 1951
Kids: Nathan, Griffin, Chelsea
Career: Actor, Voice Actor, Writer, Show Host

Mark Hamill is most famous for his role as Star Wars' iconic character, Luke Skywalker, who is in turn famous for having a galactically awful dad who ditched his mom while she was pregnant, bailed on Luke and his sister after they were born, then tried to kill Luke when he grew up after he wouldn't join his pop's evil empire and spread death and destruction for eternity. Thankfully, in real life, Mark Hamill is his on-screen father's exact opposite. He has worked hard to instill values in his kids and build strong relationships with them, and has excellent advice about keeping your eye on what's important.

Rather than expound on next-generation parenting theories and secret strategies to become a Jedi dad (though we admit, that's what we all aspire to), Hamill instead advises men to embrace the corny basics of parenting.

LOD: What were some of the core values you looked to instill in your kids as they were growing up?

MH: All the basics. It is not reinventing the wheel. Honesty, the golden rule, treating people the way you would want to be treated. All those sorts of things like kindness and selflessness, trying to do the right thing. It sounds corny when you put them into words, but I have been very lucky. It is not an easy journey. They go through the arc of life, and there could be troubling times, but you stick with it and they come through.

One of my proudest achievements is that all three of my kids and I have a great relationship. It is not easy to raise three children and not have them all have resentments or be angry at you. Keeping a strong relationship is something that you have to be dedicated to twenty-four seven.

The Takeaway: May the Force of Fatherhood Be with You

The key line that struck us when talking to Hamill was his admission that when you list all of the tried and true pieces of wisdom that have been handed down for generations, for some reason, they do sound corny or cheesy or even lame. Telling your kid to "be kind" and "treat other people how you want to be treated" over and over again sometimes feels like a cop-out because you're not bringing anything new to the table. After all, these are the same things your parents said and their parents said and their parents said, and on and on.

There has to be some new, cutting-edge knowledge you can drop on your tech-savvy, social media–wielding brood to dazzle them into being an amazing person, right? Someone, somewhere must have invented a new parenting method beyond repeatedly saying things like "honesty is the best policy." Right?

Wrong.

The reason the golden rule is still golden after millennia of kids initially rolling their eyes at it is because eventually, it seeps in and works. As Hamill says, "There is no reason to reinvent the wheel." After all, the same basic wheel concept that worked on chariots and wagons and the Model T works on your SUV. Think about it.

The Value of Smart Decision-Making
Drew Bledsoe

DADOGRAPHY

Twitter: @DrewBledsoe
Born: February 14, 1972
Kids: Stuart, John, Henry, Healy
Career: NFL Player, Entrepreneur, Winery Owner

NFL quarterbacks have to make quick, intelligent decisions to be successful when they drop back to pass the ball. Fourteen-year NFL veteran Drew Bledsoe, who was the number one pick for the New England Patriots out of the University of Washington in 1993, led the league in passing attempts three years in a row, meaning no other

QB in the league had as many lightning fast choices to make on the field. Bledsoe thrived, earning two of his four Pro Bowls during that time.

Fortunately, even though life comes at us pretty fast, it's nothing compared to a half-dozen 300-pound men looking to flatten your body into the grass in front of fifty thousand people. In that cauldron of pressure, Bledsoe relied on his coaching to make the right choice. In his life off the field, he has set up a program with his parents to help kids—his included (he has four)—learn how to make smart decisions on their own. The program is called Parenting with Dignity.

LOD: Where did the idea of Parenting with Dignity come from, and what can fathers do to help their own kids make the right choices?

DB: This is something that grew from my parents. They were both school-teachers for a bunch of years. They started working in the communities where we lived, taking skills they learned in the classroom and on the sports field and applying them to parenting. They developed a curriculum around that.

Our program really has two major messages. Number one is that when our kids make the biggest decisions in their lives, we are probably not going to be there. So our only chance is to communicate effectively our morals and our values to our kids so that they have a framework to make their own decisions.

The other major tenet that we teach is that the ideas in your head will rule your world. How you view the world will ultimately determine the decisions that you make. Our biggest defense for our kids in this big, wide world that they are going out in is to help them develop their ideas and worldview so that they can make conscious decisions.

The challenges our kids face today are totally unique. The amount of information that they have access to in the palm of their hand with a smartphone, on the Internet, and on TV is unique. They are bombarded with messages all day. If they don't have a pretty clear view of who they are and what they are about, then those influences can take over. Our biggest challenge is to try and help our kids to develop on how they see the world so that they can make the good decisions for themselves.

The Takeaway: Create a Foundation for Smart Decisions

One thought from our interview with Bledsoe really stuck out, and it was the reminder that most of the really important, split-second decisions our kids will end up making in their lives will take place without us around. Those decisions might be influenced by peer pressure, bad information, a misled desire, or any number of factors our kids will need to recognize and filter out.

We all strive to be there for our kids whenever they need anything. And many of us are. But when we aren't there and a friend is coaxing them to do something dumb or a coworker or classmate is pushing them to cheat or worse, that is when our kids will have to rely on the worldview that Bledsoe mentioned. The time spent working as a family to identify your values and understand the world around you will pay off, even if you aren't there to see it. Your reward will likely be in the bad decisions your kids *don't* make, as much as in the good decisions they do make. It's a very important lesson to keep in mind.

Three Basic Principles to Live By
John O'Hurley

DADOGRAPHY
Twitter: @ImJohnOHurley
Born: October 9, 1954
Kid: William
Career: Actor, Author, Comedian, TV Personality

For fans of *Seinfeld*, John O'Hurley will always and forever be the iconic J. Peterman, a role he embodied perfectly. He told us that during his time with Jerry and the gang, he "was lucky enough to be one of the people that held onto the belt loops of that show. That show shot to number one and they will probably be the number one show in the history of TV. It was a wonderful time. I miss the championship team and the championship season."

While we can all close our eyes and hear O'Hurley yell, "*Elaine!*" he has also voiced plenty of popular cartoon characters our kids are fans of, including King Neptune on *SpongeBob SquarePants*. As for the man behind the voice (or is it the voice from inside the man?), he became a father later in life and considers the timing of his son to be a gift. He talked to us about the pleasure of now, with his career firmly in place, having the time to just relax and watch his son's entire Little League practice, as well as his own rules for fatherhood.

LOD: When you think of your parenting philosophy, what are some things that stand out when it comes to how you're raising your son that you can share with other fathers?

JO: I think of things in three basic principles. One is to grow up and live by your imagination. I believe what we imagine is what we should be doing. I have always lived my life that way. That way, he [my son] has a fertile field in front of him and the world is a sense of infinite possibilities.

The second thing is to live contemplatively. That is, to be still. With that comes your sense of spirituality and your sense of living in that present moment and being able to appreciate the wonder of the world that is going on around you.

The final element is appreciation—the idea of recognizing the inherent vulnerability in every other human being. From that, comes the nature of being charitable, loving, and also the fact that everyone has value. All good things come from those three principles: imagination, contemplation, and appreciation. That is what I try to teach him.

For me, I say just be the kind of person you want your child to be. Children learn so much by example. Much more then we can ever teach them. They tend to correspond to what we do rather than what we say.

The Takeaway: Parenting Isn't As Difficult As Traveling the Yangtze in Search of a Mongolian Horsehair Vest

Amidst our serious efforts to instill values, work ethic, and other important traits in our kids, O'Hurley's emphasis on supporting imagination and contemplation in our kids was great to hear. These two often-overlooked traits are just as important as any other when it comes to raising thoughtful, creative kids.

How often do you set aside time for your kids (or yourself) to be creative? Or to just think? Rather than go from one practice to one activity to homework, think about setting aside some time for storytelling, creative writing, and other freewheeling mental exercises either with you or without you. Let their imaginations run wild… maybe they'll create a character as beloved as J. Peterman.

Have Enough Self-Respect to Say "Excuse Me"
Keith David

DADOGRAPHY

Twitter: @IMKeithDavid
Born: June 4, 1956
Kids: 3
Career: Actor

It took everything in our power not to name this chapter "Never Touch Another Man's Fries." For those not familiar, that is the most memorable line from one of David's most memorable characters in one of his most memorable movies, *Men at Work*. It also happens to be some of the best advice a young man can get. Even though the movie came out in 1990, David says it's still the most popular thing fans say to him when they meet him.

David has also had classic roles in *There's Something About Mary*, *Platoon*, and too many voice actor roles to count (though some dads will likely be familiar with his role as Dr. Facilier in *The Princess and the Frog*). He is the father of two daughters and while he works hard to instill them with values of kindness and fairness, as they get older, he also has a pet peeve he wants to make sure they avoid, which is spending their lives passively.

LOD: It'll be hard to top "never touch another man's fries" in terms of an iconic, perfect life lesson for kids, but if you had to pick a close second, what is something you've worked hard to make sure your daughters understand?

KD: One of the things that I insist that they do when they are walking in a crowd or even at home is to say "excuse me" if someone is in their way.

Say "excuse me." It is a great phrase. People will move out of the way if you just say "excuse me." Instead, some people will have that dumb look on their face and wait for someone to move.

I think that is the most ridiculous thing I ever had experienced in my life. You have a grown person standing there, and they won't say "excuse me." They will wait for your conversation to be over or wait until you notice them. If your back is toward them, you may not notice them. I am not spending my days thinking if someone is behind me waiting for me to move.

The Takeaway: A Simple Solution to a Simple Problem

In a day and age when kids are growing up thinking about how to get attention on social media, it's nice to hear a dad talk about the proper way to get someone's attention in the real world, politely. When kids are little and they interrupt us, we often default to the line, "Did you say excuse me?" Or if they push someone while they're trying to get somewhere, we tell them to "say excuse me." But somehow, as adults, we ask our kids to be passive (wait patiently) or overly polite (don't rush that person). Teaching them how to use a short and to-the-point phrase like "excuse me" can save them a lot of frustration and, as David says, a lot of time standing there with a dumb look on their face. Maybe it's not the most profound piece of advice—but it's certainly practical.

Taking Responsibility
Jay Wright

DADOGRAPHY

Twitter: @VUCoachJWright
Born: December 24, 1961
Kids: Reilly, Taylor, Collin
Career: College Basketball Head Coach

Villanova University head basketball coach Jay Wright led the Wildcats to two NCAA championships in 2016 and 2018, cementing his legacy as one of the best coaches of his era and putting him in the conversation amongst the best of all time. Prior to that, Wright was always thought of highly in the hoops community, but he was also thought of as the coach who may never win the big one.

In the five years leading up to the two titles, Wright's top-ranked teams were bounced early from March Madness in either the first round or the round of sixty-four. His team didn't even make the tournament in the 2011–2012 season. Rather than dodge the tough questions or blame his coaching staff or his players for the team's shortcomings, whenever pressed, Wright took full responsibility for the results and said that he had to do a better job preparing the team. End of story. The buck stopped with him.

It's no surprise, then, that Wright preaches the importance of taking responsibility to his three kids as well as all of his players.

LOD: With three kids of your own and hundreds of student-athletes who have looked up to you as a father figure over the years, what is one of the main traits you try to hammer home with your children and teams?

JW: Some of the simple lessons we talk to them about is just be a good person and to do the right thing. Take responsibility for your actions. We are not asking you to be perfect, but just take responsibility for your actions and be honest. No one is perfect. I think as a parent, you have to realize that the mistakes your kids make, we made. As long as they learn from them and take responsibility, then they will be positive experiences in their life.

You will find out that even though they [your kids] are in college, you are still parenting. You've got to do it in a different way, but you are always a part of their lives. We treat our players the same way. We treat them like family. I would tell them that what I am doing right now is what I would be doing for my own son.

There is a quote I believe that President Obama referenced in a speech after Sandy Hook: Having children is like having your heart out there running around in the world. You don't realize how everything that happens to your kids really hits you in the heart. It is probably one of the toughest things about being a parent.

You see your kids hurt and you want to protect them from everything, but sometimes you've got to realize that I've got to let them go through this. I've got to let them experience this themselves. I can't make it better for them all of the time. It is the hardest thing to do. You just don't know that you are going to be affected like that until you see your kids in those situations.

The Takeaway: Teach Your Kids to Own Their Losses the Same As Their Wins

One of the biggest clichés in sports is the idea of a coach being on the "hot seat." This typically happens when the losses begin to mount and the pressure builds and coaches need big wins to keep their job.

Coaches wind up being on the hot seat for a variety of reasons, but once a coach reaches a certain level of success, the biggest reason for game-by-game scrutiny is failure to lead a team to the promised land—meaning, a title.

Many coaches on the proverbial hot seat look for other people or circumstances to blame. Could be injuries or tough scheduling or player suspensions or anything. Not Coach Wright. Obviously, we don't fire our kids (though we may have our moments!) so they're never on the hot seat, but sometimes they go through bad patches, just like Coach Wright in the years when his teams continually came up short. Don't be afraid to own your own mistakes so your kids will see. You might not have missed a chance at a championship or lost a big game, but you might have missed a chance to attend your kid's school performance or lost an important work client. Talking to your kids about your role in these setbacks can help them see that everyone makes mistakes, and owning up to them helps you learn from them and move past them.

Model the Values You Want Your Kids to Have
John Lynch

DADOGRAPHY

Twitter: @JohnLynch49ers
Born: September 25, 1971
Kids: Leah Rose, Jake, Lillian, Lindsay
Career: NFL Player, Analyst, NFL General Manager

Strong safeties in the National Football League often set the tone for their team's entire defense. If they're hard-hitting, then the whole secondary is hard-hitting. If they're ball hawks, then the rest of the defense follows suit. When John Lynch was selected in the third round of the 1993 NFL Draft by Tampa Bay after a great college football career at Stanford University, he was ready to lead. Unfortunately, he was joining a team that, politely speaking, stunk.

His first three years with the Bucs ended in ten-loss seasons and disappointment, but along with Coach Tony Dungy and teammates like Derrick Brooks, Lynch helped turn the team into a contender. In 2002, with new coach Jon Gruden at the helm, the transformation from chumps to champions was cemented with a win in the Super Bowl.

How did they do it? Lynch and other team leaders set the example for the rest of the team to follow. Win or lose, they prepared hard, they played hard, and they gave no excuses. As more and more players bought in, the culture in Tampa changed and the wins started racking up.

Lynch, a father of four (who told us he'd have twenty kids if he could!), uses the exact same philosophy as a parent. He strives to be the model for his kids to follow.

LOD: You were a leader as a player on the field with the Bucs and Broncos, and now you're the leader of an organization with the 49ers. You're also a dad. What traits do you take from your professional career and use at home as a parent?

JL: As soon as you are a father, you will see that it is the greatest thing that you will be involved in. I really feel that. It is truly a blessing. Don't ever underestimate the responsibility that it is. I remember my father-in-law saying to me that I will be a father every day for the rest of my life. Take it seriously. It is not your words. It is your actions.

It is what you model. With my girls, I show them how a woman should be treated by the way I treat their mother. With my son, I instill in him how to treat a woman by the way I treat my wife and how I interact with my daughters. I take a lot of pride in that. I know what a tremendous responsibility it is. I know that I am not perfect at it, but I work really hard at it. It is the most fun I ever had. I think it is the coolest thing in the world.

I think one of the biggest challenges is that when you live a very public life where there is fame and fortune, how do you instill values? I'm talking about the values of hard work and how your kids will need to know that you just don't snap your fingers and have great opportunities in life. You've got to work for everything you get. Is it doable? Absolutely. Is it a challenge? Absolutely.

The Takeaway: Actively Embrace the Role of Role Model

Whether you're leading a meeting in a board room, pumping up teammates in a locker room, or talking to your kids in their bedroom, it is important to remember that what we do outside of those rooms is really what matters. Yes, the rah-rah speech or the motivational talk or the heart-to-heart discussions are important, but those are moments in time, and they are fleeting.

When we leave those talks, our consistent actions and how we conduct ourselves day in and day out will have a far greater impact on our kids than that one speech. Like Lynch said, as a father, you can give your young son one really good talk on how to treat women right and hope it sticks, or every single day he can watch how you treat your wife, daughters, female coworkers, neighbors, and friends with love and respect and know that it will sink in over time.

How to Be There for Your Kids
Bill and Willie Geist

DADOGRAPHY

Twitter: @BillGeistOne | @WillieGeist
Born: May 10, 1945 (Bill), May 3, 1975 (Willie)
Kids: 2, 2
Career: TV Hosts, News Journalists

If you've watched TV during the last forty years or so you've likely seen Bill Geist on the CBS *Evening News* or CBS Sports or even *60 Minutes II*. If you lived in New York City in the 1980s you probably read his uber-popular column in *The New York Times* called "About New York." And if you've visited any of the tourist attractions in Hollywood, you've likely walked all over Geist, or at least his star, which was placed on the Hollywood Walk of Fame in 2011.

His son, Willie Geist, followed in his father's media footsteps and is one of the cohosts of MSNBC's *Morning Joe,* as well as his own show, *Sunday Today with Willie Geist.* He is also a humorist and author of three *New York Times* bestselling books, including one he cowrote with his father, titled *Good Talk, Dad: The Birds and the Bees…and Other Conversations We Forgot to Have.*

The book was the first time the two collaborated professionally and we had the pleasure of interviewing them together.

LOD: Bill, what are some fatherhood strategies that worked for you in terms of raising a son who chose a similar career? Willie, what did you learn about being there for your kids while having a time-demanding job in the media?

BG: I would say to guide your kids in a loose fashion rather than having head-on collisions and long sit-down talks with them. I think a lot of it is in the dialogue that continues. I think that it is important to spend as much time with them as you can. There is no substitute for just time in general. When we would spend time together, I hoped that Willie would pick up cues from what I was doing.

WG: I think I got that from you too, Dad. My dad had a very busy job. He had a hard job at The New York Times. *He worked a lot. Yet somehow, he was on that bus and made it home. He coached our Little League team. I was not one of these kids that would look up in the stands and wonder where my dad was.*

BG: That was because I was on the field yelling. [They laugh.]

WG: Yeah. Well, not at me, but the umpire. You wouldn't know it because he is such a likeable, mild-mannered fellow. He was a bear in the stands. He would go after the ref. He was always there.

I do that too. There are nights where I will get frustrated if I have to go back out and do something for work. It is because that means I miss the precious three or four hours that I get with my kids in the evening and have dinner with them. So I think time spent is really it.

The Takeaway: Be There and Have Fun

There's no sense in doing everything you can to carve out time to be with your kids if you're going to take yourself too seriously. This will probably give your kids the impression that spending time with them is just another obligation, like work. During our interview with Bill, he mentioned that he made a point to laugh a lot (when he wasn't yelling at refs) while he was home and that Willie picked up his demeanor and humor from his dad. This really hits home. If you want your kids to have a great sense of humor and understand that they are a priority in your life, make it a point to be home a lot and to laugh in front of them. A lot. It may not seem like something you should have to think about, but if you're home and your mind's at work, your kids can tell. A great way to show them that your attention is where it should be is by having fun together.

One Easy Thing: Know Right from Wrong
Brian Urlacher

DADOGRAPHY

Twitter: @BUrlacher54
Born: May 25, 1978
Kids: Kennedy, Pamela, Riley
Career: NFL Player, Analyst, TV Host

There are no halls or walls of fame left for Brian Urlacher to be elected to regarding his football career. His alma mater, the University of New Mexico, recently put him on their Football Wall of Fame, and within a twelve-month span he was inducted into both the College Football Hall of Fame and the Pro Football Hall of Fame. As the heir apparent to the legendary and ferocious Chicago Bears linebackers of years past, like Dick Butkus and Mike Singletary, Urlacher's accomplishments on the gridiron are set in stone. His post-career work is still evolving, however.

After retiring from the NFL at the real-world young age of thirty-five, Urlacher quickly embraced his new role as, what he calls, "an Uber driver for my kids." Urlacher has three children (two daughters and a son) and after a decade and a half of dishing out punishment to 300-pound grownups and chasing after dudes who run 4.4 40-yard dashes, he's now content to golf (he has appeared on the Golf Channel's show *Driver vs. Driver*) and scamper after his kids.

He also partnered with author Sean Jensen for a book titled *The Middle School Rules of Brian Urlacher*, where he talks about how the challenges and experiences he had in middle school helped him become the man he is today. The book is meant to inspire kids to learn from their lives and to be their best every day by making the right decisions, which is a theme he tries to instill with his own children.

LOD: You went from running one of the most famous defenses in all of football to running your kids around town for their activities pretty quickly. Any advice for new dads in your situation?

BU: Have fun with your kids. The older they get, there is so much more you can do with them. You can golf with them. You can play basketball. You can play football. You can go fishing. It is just so much fun. Spend as much time as you can with them. It is such a fun situation to be in.

LOD: What values have you tried to teach your kids now that you're lucky enough to spend so much time with them?

BU: It is so hard these days with social media and with all the crap that is out there. I tell them that they know the difference between wrong and right. Do what is right. That is the number one thing. They understand that. They understand the difference between wrong and right like most people do. So if there is a question, do what you think is right. That is the number one thing. I try to keep them out of trouble.

The Takeaway: Simplify Your Approach When Possible

Technically, when it comes to things like instilling values in our kids and teaching them about having character or integrity, all of these traits could fall under the giant umbrella of "doing what's right." Whether it's making the right decisions or treating people well or avoiding things they know will get them in trouble, raising our kids to listen to that little voice in their heads (our voice, hopefully!) that is guiding them is important. That is clearly Urlacher's approach.

The truth is, pop culture, peer pressure, and a host of other things that exist in our kids' lives conspire to drown out that voice we've worked so hard to cultivate. Call it a conscience or a "gut feeling" or whatever you want, but our kids are hardwired with it, and we emphasize it. Our job is to guide them on how to trust that intuition and do what's right.

Cube's Rules to Live By
Ice Cube

DADOGRAPHY

Twitter: @IceCube
Born: June 15, 1969
Kids: O'Shea Jr., Karima, Deja, Shareef, Darrel
Career: Rapper, Producer, Director, Actor, Writer, Entrepreneur

Nothing marks the difference in pop culture generations between fathers and kids more starkly than what we affectionately like to call the Ice Cube Test. If the first time you became a fan of Cube was from his iconic N.W.A. album, *Straight Outta Compton*, then you're old, like us. If it was from the movie based on the iconic N.W.A. group and album, *Straight Outta Compton*, then you're probably young.

What's incredible about Cube's long and successful career is that we can run the same test with his movies. If the first time you became a fan of Ice Cube the actor was in *Boyz n the Hood* or *Friday*, then again, you're old, like us. If you saw him as a kid in *Are We There Yet?* Or *Are We Done Yet?*, then you're young.

Simple, right?

But in between Cube's careers as a rapper, actor, producer, writer, composer, director, businessman, entrepreneur, and sports league owner, he has raised four children, one of whom, O'Shea Jackson Jr., became famous playing his dad on the silver screen. When it comes to advice on fatherhood and the values he wants to instill in his kids, Ice Cube the dad is just like Ice Cube the performer. He's hard-hitting, to the point, and serious. Also smart; very, very smart.

LOD: What are some of the best pieces of wisdom you've tried to pass down to them?

IC: Mind your own business and you will live longer. Don't take (crap) from anybody. Stand up for yourself. Be nice. You don't have to be mean.

Don't leave it up to the mother to raise your kids. You need to be just as involved. Just being there is not being there. You have to be there and be involved. Don't sit on the sideline and leave it for your wife to do.

The Takeaway: Gleaming the Cube

It would be nice if every day was a good day, and we automatically raised easygoing, perfect kids—but that's not realistic for any of us. Understanding that ahead of time allows you to adopt the mindset that when you "get involved" and share the parenting responsibilities evenly, you not only share in 50 percent of the great times, but you shoulder the burden of 50 percent of the tough times too. This will help your relationship with your spouse...and your kids. When you're not on the sidelines, you can be honest and forthcoming with your kids through the good and the bad and they'll respect you more for it. In fact, Cube has consistently talked about how he didn't baby his kids as they grew up. In most cases, we agree with the "straight talk" approach with kids as well. We need to be clear about what's important so they check themselves before they wreck themselves when bad situations arise.

CHAPTER 5

Humility

"Just knowing you don't have the answers is a
recipe for humility, openness, acceptance, forgiveness,
and an eagerness to learn—and those are all good things."
—Dick Van Dyke, Father of Four

The Art of Being Grateful

Bruce Matthews

DADOGRAPHY

Twitter: @BMatthews74
Born: August 8, 1961
Kids: Jake, Kevin, Mike, Gwen
Career: NFL Player, Author

A total of five members of the Matthews clan have played in the National Football League. Starting with Clay Matthews Sr., his sons Bruce and Clay Jr., and continuing with Casey Matthews, Clay Matthews III, Kevin Matthews, and Jake, the men born into the Matthews family practically come out of the womb with college scholarship offers and NFL Draft projections. And the Matthews men aren't scrubs.

Bruce and his brother Clay Jr. each played in the league for nineteen seasons. Bruce was a fourteen-time Pro Bowler and is now a Pro Football Hall of Famer. His nephew, Clay Jr., is a Super Bowl champion and six-time Pro Bowler. Yes, genetics certainly play a role (Bruce stands about 6'5" and weighed close to 300 pounds throughout his career), but with such high expectations comes the pressure to perform and live up to your name.

Having grown up with those expectations, Bruce Matthews, a father of four, is now experiencing them on the other side of things as a dad. When it comes to people thinking you're going to be a star because of your name, or wanting to exceed the bar people have set for you, his advice to his kids is the same that his father gave him.

LOD: As one of the patriarchs of what is called the First Family of Football, what advice have you given your kids or nephews about handling the expectations heaped on them?

BM: I think the biggest thing is just being consistent. You can't say, "I am going to be the best football player" and put in all the time, doing the preparation, working out, eating right, and taking care of your body, and studying the playbook…and then go to the classroom and half-step there.

If your standard is going to be excellence, then you must be excellent in every area of your life. Whether you are going to be the best friend you can be, be the best son or daughter you can be, be the best husband or wife, or most importantly be the best parent you can be.

My dad was really simple in what his expectations were. If you start something, you don't quit. When you go out there, you give your best effort. If the coach is looking for volunteers, you step up. You be the first in line.

The big thing that I try to emphasize to my kids is that you have been blessed with an amazing opportunity to play collegiate and, for that matter, high school football. The thing that I didn't enjoy during my career was that I felt like it was always life and death. If I miss a game, my career might be over. There was always this tension about it. I don't know that I appreciated it as much as I should have. It is only in retrospect that I've come to value it a lot more. I am trying to teach my kids that.

The Takeaway: Make Your Family Name Stand for Something

While you might not have a father, brother, several sons, and a couple nephews in the NFL, your name carries its own set of expectations for your kids. For Bruce Matthews, that name means not only excellence in football but consistency and humility in all facets of life. The Matthews men don't sit back and rely on their reputation. If a coach needs something, they're taught not to act entitled, but to act with humility and volunteer first.

As dads, this made us think about what expectations our own kids will have to live up to. What key traits do we want them to associate with our family? Excellence is good. Humility is good. Consistency is good. We'll happily borrow those from the Matthews men… and then add a few of our own.

How to Show Gratitude
Denis Leary

DADOGRAPHY

Twitter: @DenisLeary
Born: August 18, 1957
Kids: John Joseph, Devin
Career: Actor, Writer, Producer, Singer, Comedian, Philanthropist

Whether ripping off fiery rants about pop culture, playing a firefighter in *Rescue Me*, or raising money for fire departments through the Leary Firefighters Foundation, Denis Leary is a scorching presence on screen, on stage, and as a fundraiser. His patented rat-a-tat-tat delivery of dialogue and comedy bits bring to mind a fighter who wears down his opponents with quick jab after quick jab before landing the haymaker, or, in Leary's case, the punch line.

Leary is a talented, Emmy-nominated actor, capable of a wide range of roles, but the persona he's most known for is the R-rated, boundary-pushing, monologue-chewing wise guy. It's all an act (well, *mostly* an act). Behind his stage-stalking presence, his incessant smoking, and his verbal machine-gun delivery lies a family man from Worcester, Massachusetts, who loves his Bruins, his Red Sox, his kids, and raising money for his favorite charities.

LOD: You're a blue-collar Boston guy at heart who has reached the height of both acting and stand-up comedy careers. Who influenced you and what lessons from your road to success have you passed along to your kids?

DL: I think it really starts with my own parents. They were extremely grateful to come to America from Ireland, and they instilled that sense of gratitude in me, as well as a responsibility to give back. These are some of the morals that I believe my own kids have because they really are great kids.

Growing up, they were able to spend a lot of time with my mother and learn about how different her childhood was in Ireland—such as spending the early years of her life without electricity. I think that went a long way toward their sense of gratitude now.

The Takeaway: Even If You're Just a Regular Joe with a Regular Job, Be Grateful

One of the hardest things to do as a parent is to explain to kids how lucky they are to be born at this point in history. The gratitude that Leary talks about learning from his own parents is extremely important to pass on to our kids because in a world where almost everything can be watched, delivered, learned, fixed, or paid for by a device that fits in the palm of our hands, our children really do need to understand that it wasn't always this way.

Whether your own parents or grandparents spent their early years without electricity like Leary's mom and dad, or you came from simple means, or you just currently aren't in a position to bring home the newest game/gadget/whatever for your kids, it's incumbent upon us to let our kids know how grateful they should be for what they have. Chances are, they have much more than other kids around the world and much more than other generations before them. If they can grow up with a sense of perspective, that's half the battle.

On Appreciation, Respect, and Courage
Curtis Martin

DADOGRAPHY

Twitter: @CurtisMartin
Born: May 1, 1973
Kids: 2 daughters
Career: NFL Hall of Famer, Philanthropist

There were two losing teams legendary NFL running back Curtis Martin did not want to play for in the early 1990s: the New England Patriots and the New York Jets. "It was in 1995," Martin told us. "They were like 1-15 or 2-14. I always associated the New England Patriots and the New York Jets with the bottom of the barrel of the NFL."

Of course, all of this was assuming he'd actually make it to pro football, which was not a sure thing considering his unfortunate injury history at the University of Pittsburgh. As a junior, Martin rushed for over 1,000 yards in ten games before he sustained a season-ending shoulder injury. He bounced back and ran for 251 yards against the University of Texas in the season opener the following year, but in the very next game against Ohio he hurt his ankle and missed the rest of the season, putting his draft status and career in doubt. Left with the decision to redshirt and try another year of college ball or declare for the NFL Draft and take his chances, he chose the latter.

When the New England Patriots selected him in the third round of the 1995 NFL Draft, all he could do was smile. Soon, Patriots fans were smiling too. Martin won Offensive Rookie of the Year and made the Pro Bowl in two of his three seasons in New England. In 1998, he signed with the other team he never wanted to play for, the New York Jets, because of his relationship with legendary coach Bill Parcells. Fourteen years later, the two would enter the Pro Football Hall of Fame together in the same class. Turned out, playing for the Pats and the Jets was the best thing that could have happened to him, and he's been wildly appreciative ever since.

As a father, Martin makes sure he includes appreciation among the values he's trying to pass down.

LOD: What are some of the core values that you look to instill in your kids as they grow up?

CM: It is hard to say which one comes first. Respect is an important value to me. I always say when your values are clear, your decisions are easy. I want to instill these values in my children and in our household so that we make the right type of decisions.

Another thing that is really, really important to me is appreciation. I make sure that my kids work for everything. I am always saying, "All right, if you do this, you can get this." I try to not just give them things. They are already going to grow up in a privileged environment. I didn't have that luxury. I really liked what the struggle has taught me. In my situation, I somewhat have to create a struggle for my children so that they can appreciate a dollar and they can appreciate life.

So appreciation, respect, and courage are huge values for me. I always tell people that whatever you fear in life creates your boundaries. So if a person fears heights, they are going to stay on the ground. If they fear flying, they are going to drive everywhere. I feel like we have a very courageous family. I would like for my kids to be kids and enjoy themselves. I really like to have fun. Not only with my kids but myself. I want them to have a fun personality, but those are the three core values.

The Takeaway: Don't Fumble Opportunities Because of Fear

If someone had told twenty-year-old Curtis Martin that the only two teams he'd play for in the NFL would be the "bottom of the NFL barrel" Patriots and Jets, and that he'd have a Hall of Fame career playing on those teams, he never would have believed it. Those teams weren't good, and he was afraid he'd be stuck in a no-win situation if he played in either city.

Now, think about all the opportunities we close off in our own minds as parents when it comes to our kids. We often assume they wouldn't enjoy something or like a place or have an interest in an activity because of our own thoughts or experiences on the subject—but just like Martin, you have to remember one thing: you could be dead wrong. Have the courage to support your kids and let them draw their own conclusions.

Having Compassion and Sensitivity
Titus Welliver

DADOGRAPHY

Twitter: @Welliver_Titus
Born: March 12, 1961
Kids: Quinn, Eamonn, Cora
Career: Actor, Producer

Titus Welliver's rise—from his first credited film role of "Redneck in a Bar" in the 1990 movie *Navy SEALs* starring Charlie Sheen to leading man in Amazon's *Bosch* TV series—has been a study in persistence and perseverance. During the early part of his career, he survived on bit parts and one-offs, often appearing in a single episode of a TV series or for a single scene in a movie. For avid TV watchers, he was one of "those guys" who you instantly recognized from a memorable small role in another show.

Like a baseball player, Welliver thrived on hitting singles and doubles for a while, getting multi-episode roles on shows like *NYPD Blue* and even starring roles on a few shows that only lasted a season or so. By the time he landed a recurring role on HBO's hit series *Deadwood,* he was an acting veteran who would soon appear in some of the biggest movies (*The Town, Argo, Gone Baby Gone*) and TV shows (*The Good Wife, Sons of Anarchy, Lost*).

Through it all, Welliver relied on his father's advice to handle his success and to help him raise his three children.

LOD: Hollywood isn't exactly known for being the nicest business, but being thoughtful and treating people right is clearly important to you. Are those the most important traits you want your kids to have?

TW: I have three children. I have my daughter Cora, my son Quinn, and my son Eamonn. Something that I focus on very, very deeply is compassion for other human beings, sensitivity to other human beings, and kindness. They also should have gratitude for what they have, and I don't just mean material things.

I find that I become my father when I find my kids not eating everything off their plate. I can't believe that I even said that, but I do go to that place. I think it is important to say that there are people starving on this planet. They would crawl to get that one little piece of meat or that one vegetable that they [my kids] refuse to eat. We are blessed to be able to have these things. These are things that I think we take for granted. I think it is very important to remind our children that they need to have gratitude. Not just for, say, their bike, but things that are taken for granted. They can drink clean water. They can take a hot bath. They don't live in a place where they have to be fearful all the time.

As my father used to say, I try and instill good morals in my children. I tell my kids to always tell the truth because it is the easiest thing to remember. That is tricky because kids like to fib. Still, I have three amazing children. When people ask me about my accomplishments in life, I say that the best accomplishment in my life is that I have three amazing children that I love without measure. They inspire me. They fulfill me. That is everything. That is really everything.

The Takeaway: It's Okay to Steal Your Parents' Best Lines

Titus Welliver spends his days reciting lines written for him by some of the best scribes in Hollywood, and when he's home at night, in his own house, he finds himself reciting lines his father said decades earlier. If a professional actor eschews professional wordsmithing for good, old-fashioned parenting morals and phrases, you should feel comfortable about doing the same.

We all remember when we were kids and our parents told us not to waste food because someone in some far-off country was starving and would love to have what we have. We all remember rolling our eyes too. Now we're parents and we're saying the same thing. Maybe there's something to it. Maybe it's called teaching gratitude.

It's Always Good to Stay Humble
Charlie Ward

DADOGRAPHY

Twitter: @RealCharlieWard
Born: October 12, 1970
Kids: Caleb, Hope, Joshua
Career: Heisman Memorial Trophy Winner, NBA Player, Author

It's rare in modern athletics to accomplish something that nobody in the history of sports has done, but Florida State University legend and New York Knicks icon Charlie Ward has achieved just that. He is the only athlete to ever win college football's Heisman Trophy and also play in an NBA Finals (he was actually a starter). Also, he won a college football national championship with the Florida State Seminoles in 1993. So, yeah, he's in a club of one.

Even more amazing is that in each sport, football and basketball, Ward played the most important position on each team: quarterback and point guard. In both roles, Ward has the ball in his hands the majority of the time, and it's up to him to run the team's offense, be a coach on the field or floor, and set the tempo for his squad as a leader.

While many would expect a person with Ward's accomplishments and responsibilities to be loud and brash and bold, his demeanor was the exact opposite. He was quiet, measured, and always cool. He led almost exclusively by example. As he has transitioned out of pro sports into a role as a coach, and as he's raised his own children, he has remained humble and tried to pass on that quality.

LOD: You're in a league of your own when it comes to your athletic accomplishments, but the way you've handled your success is what also sticks with people. When you talk to your own kids or your players, what are some traits you hope they pick up by watching you?

CW: Humility is certainly one. Having character and integrity are also very important. I also talk about being honest. I'd say having a strong work ethic is another one. It's also critical for kids to learn to have the courage to make decisions and live with those decisions. Every choice has a consequence, whether it is positive or negative. Those are the things that we are looking to instill into our kids.

The truth is, they are going to make bad decisions, like we all do from time to time. We just don't want them to make costly decisions or the same bad choices over and over again. Occasionally, young people don't think through their environment or about the quality of their friends, and those things have consequences that may hurt them in the long term. Whether it is on the Internet or if they are doing something inappropriate, we have been able to help them work through those challenges as they grow up. It goes a long way to the success that you have. Having integrity. Being honest. Those things will help you long term.

The Takeaway: Give Cockiness "the Heisman"

We all know that the loudest and most colorful athletes tend to get the most attention—especially from our kids. One of Charlie Ward's fellow Seminole legends, Deion Sanders, is a great example. But you can win and lead just as easily with quiet confidence and calm under pressure. Ward is a great example of that.

The next time your kids want to idolize the player who shows up his opponents and makes a scene on the sideline, sit your kids down and let them watch Ward's highlights on *YouTube*. They'll see someone electrify 100,000 people in Tallahassee and make a capacity crowd at Madison Square Garden erupt with joy…all while being tough, physical…and humble.

CHAPTER 6

Wisdom

"Where wisdom reigns, there is no conflict
between thinking and feeling."
—Carl Jung, Father of Five

How to Win the Balancing Battle
Jim Gaffigan

DADOGRAPHY

Twitter: @JimGaffigan
Born: July 7, 1966
Kids: Jack, Patrick, Marre, Katie Louise, Michael
Career: Comedian, Actor, Writer, Producer

"Male model. Long snapper." The beginning of comedian Jim Gaffi-gan's *Twitter* bio says it all…since he's neither of those things. As for the model part, well, his first book was titled *Dad Is Fat*. Regarding being a long snapper, Gaffigan did play football at Georgetown University, but he was an offensive lineman. But we don't hold it against him. When it comes to the most important topics—parenthood, family, and his legendary bits on Hot Pockets and McDonald's—he sticks to the truth…at least the comedic version of it. And he's got plenty to tell.

Gaffigan is a *New York Times* bestselling author, one of the top stand-up comedians in the country, an actor, and the father of five kids. He routinely travels for work, so his thoughts on staying in touch with his kids, bringing them on tour, and how to keep tabs on everything clearly provide fodder for his comedy. However, he carefully measures his dad joke time on stage. We'll let him explain: "Well, when I started about twenty years ago, I would see comedians talk about their wife and kids. I remember sitting in the audience going, 'That is great—I can't even get a date. I don't know what you are talking about.'"

At *Life of Dad*, we love his entire routine, but his bits on fatherhood especially resonate.

LOD: You have five kids. People seem to make this a topic of conversation all the time. What is your response, and what is your strategy for staying involved with all your children?

JG: I think the biggest adjustment was two kids. At least for me. There is an asterisk next to that because I am a guy who travels a lot doing stand-up comedy. I get this forced one- or two-day break every week.

I think it is very fascinating how everyone is really curious about how everyone else is going to procreate. It is baffling! You would never ask someone when they are getting their hair cut. People are consumed with curiosity. If a couple is married or dating for longer than six months, people suddenly need to know whether they are going to have a baby.

I don't care; I just think it is funny. I know that we have had way beyond the normal amount of children. People are like, "Are you going to have any more children?" I am like, "Why do you care? Are you going to pay for their college? How is that any of your business?" This myth of overpopulation comes from eighteenth-century England, and no one wants to admit that it's just BS. People don't ask why someone owns two cars. Why does anyone else care? I say, "Don't worry, I am taking care of this."

For strategy, I think it is an ongoing process of checking in. The fact that you are in charge of another human being's development is overwhelming. For me, it is a constant battle of keeping a balance between work and parenting. I think that we have found a good balance with me doing stand-up. I am lucky enough to do theaters, and I can travel with my kids on the tour bus.

Even writing [books] took me away from parenting responsibilities that I think are pretty important. It is not about going to birthday parties. It is about being there when they go to the doctor. I think it is going beyond ordering pizza and going to dance recitals. I want to be involved to a certain level.

It was interesting writing the book. In the end, I remember thinking, "If no one buys the book, at least if my kids eventually ever read it, they would say, 'He was thinking a lot about parenting. He was not perfect, but he tried.'"

The Takeaway: You Don't Have to Be Perfect, but You Have to Try

You may have five kids or you may have one, but the strategy Gaffigan mentions (even though he's being self-deprecating) is the same. Show your kids that you care. There is no such thing as a model dad. There's no such thing as a dad who can be present for every important (and unimportant) moment in their kids' lives. But when you are there, give your kids your full attention and let them know you care however you can.

And since you probably don't have your own tour bus, find other ways to get your kids occasionally involved with your work. It'll be good for them to see what you do while they're at school and it'll give them a greater appreciation for your responsibilities as they get older.

Hunker Down, Be There, and Get It Done
Scott Fujita

DADOGRAPHY

Twitter: @SFujita55
Born: April 28, 1979
Kids: Isabell, Delilah, Marlowe
Career: NFL Player, Producer

When Hurricane Katrina made landfall on the Gulf Coast at the end of August 2005, it was a Category 3 storm with 100- to 140-mile-per-hour winds. The storm caused severe devastation and the catastrophic aftermath left a majority of New Orleans flooded, causing roughly $100 billion in damage, including shutting down the city's sports mecca, the Superdome.

Roughly a year later, on September 25, 2006, with the city and the nation having bestowed the NFL's New Orleans Saints as the barometer of the region's recovery, the team would pull off one of the most symbolic wins in sports history, led by Drew Brees on offense, Scott Fujita on defense, and Steve Gleason on special teams.

That Fujita was involved, not only as the team's captain and leader in tackles but as one of the team's leading philanthropists, makes sense. Civic duty and social responsibility is in his bones. The roster of organizations he supports and charities he's involved in include causes supporting the environment, equal rights, cancer research, community organization, and many more. He was also heavily involved with the award-winning documentary *Gleason,* about his teammate's battle against Lou Gehrig's disease (ALS).

Fujita has three children and while he shares his own thoughts on fatherhood, he has also learned several things on the topic from watching his friend Steve Gleason fight so valiantly.

LOD: What are some things you've learned from not only your football career but your career giving back to your community and being involved with Team Gleason that you'd like to pass down to your children?

SF: I always say no matter how many parenting books you have read, nothing prepares you for when those kids are dropped into your arms. So here we are with two newborn twins looking at each other like, "Okay, now what?" You just hunker down and get it done. There are really no words that you can use to describe what it means to be a parent and what the feeling is like until you actually experience it and feel it. There is no better calling in the world.

One of my favorite quotes, and I saw this in The Contender, *is that principles only mean something if you stick by them when they're inconvenient. My goal is to raise confident, strong kids who have principles and who are willing to stand up for those principles—whatever they may be. I don't want to guide them so strictly and tell them what they should and shouldn't believe. I want them to have their own backbones and deep principles and be willing to stand up for them.*

I think the message from Steve is how to be more present and not take these moments for granted. I love the guy as a friend. We have a lot of history, but I am so proud of him as a father. I know that his example, without question, is making me become a better dad. Some of the messages that we have heard from people who have seen [Gleason] are things like, "I lost touch with my son in the past few years—I am going to pick up the phone and give him a call." Or a parent that might say after dinner that they're going to put the computer or phone down and spend more time with their kids. Those are all the things that I think are striking a chord with the viewers. From a parenting standpoint, the documentary is very authentic.

The Takeaway: Have a Sense of the Moment

Whether Fujita was standing in the rebuilt Superdome after Hurricane Katrina, in the hospital room after having twin girls, or beside his good friend Steve Gleason, his sense of the present and what's important is admirable. Having been a part of such impactful moments and been involved with so many impressive individuals has clearly affected him, and it's a good reminder for all of us to take stock of the people important to us and the situations we're in. Are were present for those who need us? Are we putting our kids and their concerns ahead of our own? Are we actively thinking of ways to help?

What to Say Before Bedtime
Brad Meltzer

DADOGRAPHY

Twitter: @BradMeltzer
Born: April 1, 1970
Kids: 2 sons, 1 daughter
Career: Author, TV Host, Comic Book Writer

Author Brad Meltzer is the literary version of baseball's five-tool player. He writes bestselling thrillers, nonfiction books, children's books, comic books, and televisions scripts. Oh, he's also hosted a few TV shows on the History channel. So maybe he's a six-tool player? Suffice to say, Meltzer is one of the most prolific and successful writers around today, covering a wide variety of interests and topics, from political conspiracies to his Ordinary People Change the World books.

When we spoke to Meltzer, he was promoting that series, which he created as a way for his kids to read about and become interested in heroes, rather than modern-day celebrities who seek fame. He explains it like this: "I wrote these books because I was tired of my kids looking at reality TV show stars and big-mouth athletes and thinking that they are heroes. That is being famous. To me, being famous is a lot different than being a hero. I was determined to give them real heroes." The heroes he has written about so far include Abraham Lincoln, Jane Goodall, Amelia Earhart, Martin Luther King Jr., Albert Einstein, Helen Keller, and over a dozen more. In addition to these books, he wrote the acclaimed *Heroes for My Daughter* and *Heroes for My Son*.

LOD: We love that you are able to bounce back and forth between writing gripping thrillers for adults and then entertaining and informative stories for kids. Have you pulled any quotes or phrases from your work or research that you've passed along to your children as a mantra or motto?

BM: Every night that I tuck my kids into bed, I say the same three things to them: Dream big. Work hard. Stay humble. Every night. When I say "Dream big and work hard," they say, "Stay humble." It is like Friday Night Lights *in our house.*

I got it from a friend whose dad told him that years ago. I just love it. In fact, I did an entire TED Talk on that ("Write Your Story, Change History"). It is the most popular TED Talk that I have done. I think it is because other people want similar values for their kids.

I think that there is only one rule when it comes to being a parent as far as I am concerned. It is love your kids. You can screw up everything else. We are all going to give bad advice and good advice. As long as you love your kids and your kids feel that love, they will figure it out.

The Takeaway: *Friday Night Lights* and Good Nights

Fine, we'll just say it. We're stealing the "Dream big. Work hard. Stay humble." line and using it with our own kids. It's simple and perfect and encapsulates so much of what we all try to instill in our kids. Also, we love the idea that as parents, we say the first part and our kids finish the phrase. That method reaffirms that it's going to be "our phrase" rather than something we preach to them.

Of course, once they're on a team, we can use "Clear eyes. Full hearts. Can't lose." That's pretty good, too, and we don't want to tick off Coach Taylor.

Explaining Blackberry Moments and Making Kids Feel Special
Ernie Johnson

DADOGRAPHY

Twitter: @TurnerSportsEJ
Born: August 7, 1956
Kids: Michael, Carmen, Maggie, Ashley, Eric, Allison
Career: Broadcaster, Author

Everyone loves Ernie Johnson.

It's true. Shaquille O'Neal, Charles Barkley, and Kenny Smith, his cohosts on TNT's *Inside the NBA*, will tell anyone who listens how great he is (when they're not poking fun at him, of course). In praise for Johnson's book about his life as a father, son, husband, and man of faith, *Unscripted: The Unpredictable Moments That Make Life Extraordinary*, Barkley sums up his feelings about "EJ" by saying, "Ernie is quite simply one of the best people on the planet."

While so many people know Johnson as the three-time Emmy-winning TV host, his life off the screen is vastly more impressive. He is a cancer survivor. He is the father of six children (he adopted four of them). He's a grandfather. He has been presented with several lifetime achievement awards from his alma mater, the University of Georgia. His list of accolades and accomplishments goes on and on. However, during our very candid discussion with Johnson about marriage, fatherhood, and family, what was most impressive was how he sugarcoats nothing. Adopting kids was hard. Fighting cancer was hard. Parenting can be hard. But in the end, as his book says, that's what makes life extraordinary.

LOD: You refer to a phrase you've coined—"blackberry moments"—in your book that all parents and kids could bring into their own lives. Can you share where that idea came from and explain it a bit?

EJ: I hope people latch on to that concept because it came from many years ago, as I explained in the book. It was during a Little League game that we had to stop for a moment because a couple of our fielders jumped over a fence to get a ball. They had forgotten about the ball and were eating blackberries that were growing behind the fence. As so often happens as you get older and you think about experiences in your life, some of them take on added meaning. That one was one of those.

It was an amusing story for us when we were growing up, talking about the day that it happened. I then thought about the times that we get so preoccupied with the game—whether "the game" is our job, the next conference call, or the next responsibility. We get these blinders on and we don't use our peripheral vision and say, "Wow, there are some blackberries growing here. I am going to take a minute and enjoy them."

There are a lot of the moments that God puts out there for us, but if we are so into our smartphone, we might miss them. If I have a pet peeve, it is when I am looking around the workplace or wherever I am and see people just buried in their phones. You miss so much that is right in front of you if you do that. You can impact someone else's life or they can impact yours if you are not so tied up in the game.

The Takeaway: Look Out for Blackberry Moments

While the phrase used to be "stop and smell the roses," we here at *Life of Dad* are much more comfortable with, "hop a fence during a Little League game and eat some blackberries." It is the perfect visual and perfect metaphor for the point that Johnson is trying to illustrate. As fathers with our own careers and interests and responsibilities outside of our role as parents, we're all guilty of checking our phones too much, or being present physically while we're mentally working on a project or thinking of an upcoming event.

The next time you feel yourself drifting away from the present, think of EJ and his blackberry moments and snap out of it. Your kids will notice and do the same.

Using Sports to Teach Life Lessons
Grant Hill

DADOGRAPHY

Twitter: @RealGrantHill33
Born: October 5, 1972
Kids: Myla Grace, Lael
Career: NBA Player, Analyst

For a five-year stretch in the late 1990s, Grant Hill lived in rarified basketball air. He won two national championships at Duke University for legendary coach Mike Krzyzewski, was selected as an All-American, and then was drafted third overall in the 1994 NBA Draft. Over the next eight years, he'd win an Olympic gold medal, make seven NBA All-Star teams, four All-NBA second teams, and one All-NBA first team. He was one of the most marketable and most likeable players the association had and seemed to be headed for all-time greatness. Unfortunately, he suffered from ongoing injuries. He managed to battle back and return to the league, playing admirably until the 2013 season, but he never regained his previous form.

Hill is now a member of the Naismith Memorial Basketball Hall of Fame and part owner of the Atlanta Hawks. One of the traits that made Hill so popular during his playing career was his sterling image and integrity. His answers during most interviews were well thought out, and whether he was promoting his favorite charity or working as a spokesman for Sprite, he displayed charisma and character. When asked about his influences, he credits his father (who played in the NFL) and his mother, and sports in general for teaching him about life. As a father of two, he continues to lean on athletics to instill life lessons.

LOD: You've been around sports all of your life. What lessons do you take from your father, Calvin Hill, Coach K, and other coaches to pass along to your own kids?

GH: Coach K taught me that there are so many values that you can take from the game [basketball] and apply to life. There is hard work. There is preparation, discipline, collective responsibility, and pride. All these different things that he stressed makes him a great coach, teacher, and a leader. It also translated into great teams.

Not all of his teams win the championship, but for the most part they play and do things the right way. I think a lot of those values you can take with you off the court. I know I have. It stuck with me. I was a teenager, twenty-some-odd years ago, playing for Coach K, but I still think about those lessons and apply them in all facets of life.

Sometimes in life, you get caught up in trying to achieve and get ahead. In sports, sometimes you get a bit narcissistic. You worry about your legacy and your impact. I really feel ultimately that you are judged upon how your children turn out. What kind of people they are, what kind of values they have, and are they productive citizens, if you will. It is important as a parent to be engaged and involved. I was fortunate to have some great parents. They set the bar pretty high. For my wife and I, it is all about the kids.

The Takeaway: There's No Substitute for Team Sports

As Hill said, the values children learn from athletics in general and team sports in particular carry over into society on nearly every level. Learning the value of hard work, preparation, dedication, responsibility, and pride—all while being physically and mentally active—makes sports a great outlet for kids, even if it's only a passing interest when they're younger.

You can support your kids' foray into sports by offering positive feedback and encouragement, and backing up the coach's lessons. Your kids will learn a lot…even if they're not in a locker room with Coach K at Cameron Indoor Stadium.

Putting Family First
Stephen Amell

DADOGRAPHY

Twitter: @StephenAmell
Born: May 8, 1981
Kid: Maverick
Career: Actor, Entrepreneur, WWE Wrestler

For a guy who grew up loving comic books and professional wrestling, Stephen Amell has found himself quite literally living the dream. He is currently the star of The CW's hit series *Arrow*, and he's even made a few guest appearances on WWE's *Monday Night Raw*. Known for his athleticism and energy, Amell is drawn to physical roles that allow him to break a sweat and even more importantly, perform his own stunts. He put his fitness skills to the test on *American Ninja Warrior*, and the video of him crushing the course has racked up more than eleven million views.

With so many interests and career opportunities at his fingertips, Amell admitted to us that for a brief period of time, he lost track of what was important and he chased some things that may not have been in his best interest. These days, he has things in the exact order that he wants them, and for that, he can thank his daughter. "Once she was born, it really made life so much simpler," he says. "I say that to people and they look at me sideways because they think kids are so much work. Obviously, they are. At the same time, at points in my career I feel like my priorities got out of whack. Now she is my number one priority at all times. That will never change. It then becomes way easier to slot everything else where it should be in your life."

LOD: You grew up loving superheroes, and now you're playing one on TV. What is the number one trait you'd take from that world or your own experience and pass along to your daughter?

SA: I just want her to be honest. There are going to be things that she is going to experience in the world today that I am not totally going to understand. So I can only imagine that five years or ten years from now, kids are going to be into different stuff, and technology is going to be in a spot where it is moving faster than I am capable of understanding. I just want her to always be able to come and talk to me and have open conversations. Just because she might get into something that I don't approve of doesn't mean we can't talk about why I don't approve. I just hope that she will view me as someone who she can trust and confide in.

LOD: What is the best piece of parenting advice you've ever been given?

SA: The greatest piece of parenting advice was from my father-in-law. He looked at me one day. This was after about four bourbons. He goes, "Junior." (He calls me Junior. I don't know why.) He said, "You get what you expect." I thought that was the best piece of parenting advice that I have ever gotten. You get what you expect.

The Takeaway: Priorities Are Everything

We all chase things. We chase our dreams, we chase opportunities, we chase hobbies, and sometimes we fall into the trap that if we just chase and catch one more thing, we'll be slightly happier or more fulfilled or content or at peace.

Nope.

When your priorities are in order, as Amell says, you can quit the chase and focus on what truly matters. Your kids. Your family. Your passions. With those as your bedrock, the chase can end and your best life can truly begin.

The Five Principles of Fatherhood
Allan Houston

DADOGRAPHY

Twitter: @Allan_Houston
Born: April 20, 1971
Kids: 7
Career: NBA Player, General Manager

We admit that when we set out to interview Allan Houston about his basketball career with the New York Knicks, his outstanding college career at the University of Tennessee (playing for his dad, Wade), and his Father Knows Best retreat for dads, we didn't expect to have him quote Confucius to us. But he did, and it made sense. When talking about the family-building curriculum of his foundation, he said the Chinese teacher from 500 B.C. put it best: "To put the world in order, we must put the nation in order. To put the nation in order, we must put the family in order."

In terms of family, Houston is the patriarch of a large one. He has seven children, and with each of them he strives to duplicate the special relationship he has with his own father. He firmly believes (and rightly so) that there are near countless benefits that can be reaped in society and in individual households when fathers are involved, equal participants in their children's lives. The main focus of his foundation's retreats is to give fathers and their children uninterrupted quality time to bond, talk, and perhaps discuss things that they may not in the course of their day-to-day lives.

LOD: Your program for dads has an official five principles of fatherhood. Can you share those with us?

AH: The five principles of our fatherhood program are faith, integrity, sacrifice, leadership, and legacy. Within those five frames, we make sure we know what is right and try to move in that direction. We want our kids to be hard workers. We don't want them to take anything for granted. Whatever dime we make, we want to earn it. We can all lead. We don't want them to be followers. You can be laid back or you can be intense, but you can still lead.

Then we talk about legacy. My grandfather is ninety years old. We still get to see and talk to him. We want to make sure our kids understand the legacy our parents and grandparents left. We want them to recognize that and understand that. So for the morals, we try to use the five principles in the fatherhood program for our kids as they grow up.

The Takeaway: Use Allan Houston's Five Principles or Create Your Own

One of the themes we've noticed throughout our interviews with *Life of Dad* is that fathers like to quantify their parenting philosophies. Some dads call them "mottos" or "beliefs" or "rules" or, like Houston, "principles," but whatever they are, they're in a list, they're well thought out, and they provide a foundation for wisdom and guidance.

The next time you find yourself with a few spare minutes, we recommend jotting down five bullet points that would encapsulate what you could call your personal dad rules. Keep each one to a few words or a sentence at most. Keep it with you or on your phone and revisit it and revise it as needed. When the time comes, you can pass it on to your own children. Now that's a legacy.

Keep an Open Mind
Darryl McDaniels

DADOGRAPHY

Twitter: @TheKingDMC
Born: May 31, 1964
Kid: Darryl Jr.
Career: Rapper, Entrepreneur, Comic Book Writer

Hip-hop legend Darryl McDaniels, better known as DMC (Devastating Mic Control), was one-third of arguably the most influential rap group in the genre's history. Along with Joseph "Rev Run" Simmons and Jason "Jam Master Jay" Mizell, the three musicians from Hollis, Queens, redefined what rap superstardom could be. From their iconic beats to their Adidas affiliation to their boundary-bashing collaboration with Aerosmith and even to their holiday classic, "Christmas in Hollis," Run-DMC pushed boundaries.

McDaniels was originally a DJ, but after some urging from Run to grab the microphone and start rapping, DMC was born. Since that time, McDaniels has been a creative force, rapping on numerous number one tracks and most recently starting his own comic book imprint.

Not to be overlooked in all of his commercial successes are the amazing things McDaniels has done behind the scenes for foster care and the promotion of adoption. When McDaniels was thirty-five, his mother revealed to him that he had been adopted and that his birth mother put him up for adoption when he was three months old. After a thorough search, he reunited with his birth mom and has become a strong advocate for adoption, so much so that he was recently presented with an Angels in Adoption award by the Congressional Coalition on Adoption Institute.

McDaniels has one son, who he says above all else, he teaches to be honest. He also hammers home how important it is to have an open mind. In our interview with him, he tells a phenomenal story about how the biggest hit record of his career almost didn't happen because he was being close-minded. We'll let him tell it.

LOD: You learned your lesson about the importance of keeping an open mind at the height of your career when producing "Walk This Way." Can you share that story?

DM: When we first made the record "Walk This Way," the way you all heard it, me and Run didn't like it. Now, this is how it went down. Originally, Jay and I were going to sample "Walk This Way." Run and I were supposed to talk about how good we are:

"I'm DMC in the place to be. Been rhymin' on the mic since '83. I'm the best MC in history. There will never be an MC better than me." Then Run was going to say, "I'm DJ Run and I'm number one."

Rick Rubin came into the studio and told us we should do the record over. Run and I were thinking from a limited hip-hop point of view. We told Rick that we are going to sample it. We are going to rhyme over it. That is doing it over.

Rick said that we should do it the way Aerosmith had originally done it. Jay had heard the record past the break in the song. Run and I never heard the record past the break. So Rick gave us the record and told us to let it play. Take down a pen and paper and write down the lyrics on the record so you can learn them.

When we heard Steven's voice we were like, "Oh, hell no!" This is hillbilly gibberish. You guys are taking this rock/rap stuff way too far. You are going to ruin our careers. Afrika Bambaataa and the Zulu Nation are going to hate us. You are going to make us the laughin' stock of the music industry. We said, "We are not doing this!"

There was a fight until Jay and Rick were able to convince us to come to the studio. They said to do the lyrics the way Steven is singing them. Run and I were pissed off. We were screaming. Jay said, "Do the record like Run and D would do it." It was almost like Diff'rent Strokes with Arnold saying, "Whatcha talkin' 'bout, Willis?" We said, "Whatcha talkin' 'bout, Jay?" He said to do the signature switch off and do the lyrics by helping each other out. So we did that. He put Steve on the last vocal. That is the version that you hear today.

When we heard the finished product, it was cool. It was funky. The vocals, the delivery, and Joe Perry's guitar riffs are tight. Steven's vocals were tight. The moral of that story is always be open to try something new because not only will it change your life but it could change the world.

The Takeaway: It's Tricky—but Keep an Open Mind

Depending on your kids' age, they may or may not be ready just yet for a music/life lesson involving "Walk This Way." When they're ready, and you pull up the video on *YouTube*, explain the importance of the video at the time and the lasting impact of the song, and then tell them it almost didn't happen because DMC and Run were being stubborn...well...once they fall in love with the song, your point about keeping an open mind should be made.

Enjoy the Moment
Brett Dalton

DADOGRAPHY

Twitter: @IMBrettDalton
Born: January 7, 1983
Kid: Sylvia
Career: Actor

Actor Brett Dalton loves to play the bad guy. He relishes it. In his starring role as Grant Ward on Marvel's *Agents of S.H.I.E.L.D.*, he got to play the ultimate heel, seemingly working as a member of the good guys (S.H.I.E.L.D.) but secretly working for the villains (Hydra). On set, he got to chop it up with the late, great Bill Paxton and also experiment with some killer lines and diabolical schemes to take over the world. And while all of this sinister bravado is very "in character" for his character, it is completely out of character for the real-life Dalton, who is a doting, caring, and kind father.

He's just as likely to be singing the *Frozen* soundtrack (for the five-hundredth time) in the car years after the movie came out as he is to be dancing with his daughter around the house. In our conversation with him, Dalton shared his opinions on giving your kids space, talking to them with real words and not baby-voice words (even when they're a baby), and learning how to enjoy moments rather than hold onto them too tightly.

LOD: Your enthusiasm for being a dad has come through our whole conversation. What are some unique tips and strategies that you'd recommend to other parents if they asked you for advice?

BD: We try to have respect for where [my daughter] is at as a human being at this particular point. We have never done the baby voice. We have never said "no" without an explanation. We try and explain things to her. We try to have patience and sympathy for where she is at in her process of this crazy world that we brought her into. So we just try and talk to her like a human being. We also have been very lucky as well. She didn't have colic or anything like that. It kind of felt like she was meant to be. She didn't even cry when she was born. She had this look on her face like, "Oh, this is what I imagined the world to be like. This is cool."

You also have to let them be who they are. You have a child that you brought into this world—another living being who wouldn't be here if it wasn't for you. There is a lot of responsibility there. You are filled with love for this little being. There is a tendency to want to be a helicopter parent. You want to solve everything for them. You want to see them happy. You would do anything in the world to make your children happy. For instance, tying their shoelace. Let them figure it out. I feel that if you are always helping them, it creates a dependency.

Let them be who they are and you don't have to hold onto moments with a clutched fist. It is with an open hand. You have to let them discover things as they go. You can be there for their protection, of course. (Obviously, if they are playing with knives, step in.) If they are having issues with tying their shoe, what are the consequences? Let them figure it out. Then they will have a sense of accomplishment. That goes a long way.

The Takeaway: Don't Over-S.H.I.E.L.D. Your Kids

We were really impressed with Dalton's take on letting kids figure things out for themselves, even at a young age. Using his shoe-tying example is meaningful because we've all been there. Sure, sometimes it's urgent because our kid needs to make the bus or leave for an appointment, and we have to hurry things along…

But outside of those instances, it's okay to let them get frustrated and fail a few times. When they finally can do it by themselves, the sense of accomplishment they'll have and the confidence to do it again next time will be worth the wait.

Embracing the Joy of Going the Father Route
Jim Breuer

DADOGRAPHY

Twitter: @JimBreuer
Born: June 21, 1967
Kids: Dorianne, Kelsey, Gabrielle
Career: Comedian, Actor, Musician, Radio Host

You want fatherhood advice from Goat Boy? Or how about a man-to-man dad talk with Joe Pesci? Only one guy can offer you both: *Saturday Night Live* alumnus and stand-up comedian Jim Breuer. Breuer, who also does spot-on impressions of Jack Nicholson, Sly Stallone, and other Hollywood legends, tells us that even with all of his comedy, podcast, and album success, he still doesn't feel like he "made it, made it."

"I really don't," he says. "I felt like I was on track when I got a TV show before *Saturday Night Live*. It was called *The Uptown Comedy Club*. Tracy Morgan was on it. That was when I felt like I was on track to making it. With *SNL* and *Half Baked*, I thought I was going to make $10 million a year in movies. I thought I would be wearing leather pants. I would have a kangaroo in the yard. I thought I would be shipping creatures in from Africa. I thought I would have a puma in there. It didn't happen. I didn't want to move to L.A., and that probably hurt. I didn't want to. I started a family. When my daughter was two years old, I really thought it would be best to be home and close to her for other reasons. I took the father route."

Here at *Life of Dad*, we're clearly not going to argue with anyone for taking the "father route," and we applaud his decision. Breuer, for his part, doesn't regret it for one second. He is the proud dad of three daughters and believes that having kids can put your whole life into the proper perspective.

LOD: How excited were you about becoming a dad, and what do you tell guys you meet on tour who are thinking of becoming fathers?

JB: I couldn't wait. I couldn't get enough of the anticipation. It was so exciting. I loved the entire process of being with my wife. I couldn't wait to be a father. The minute my daughter was born, it just came natural. I loved taking over. I love sacrificing a lot of time, touring, and work just so I could be with the children. I love doing that. I enjoy doing that. I always feel like I should give more. Others might say that I am out of my mind.

There is a guy that I brought on tour with me. His wife wants a child. He is like, "Sure, I just can't wait to throw my money out the door. All my time will just go to a baby. That should be fun!"

I told him, "Let me explain it this way. When you have a child—and I don't care what you have accomplished in your life—usually about four to six months into parenthood, you sit and go what the hell were we doing in life up until this moment? What a blur and what a waste."

[Before having kids] we would be like, "Hey, it's Friday night. Let's get high and wasted and watch a show." It is just so irrelevant. It is a blur, gray blob of just no importance whatsoever. It is like, "Just gonna watch reruns of 3rd Rock from the Sun. I just found this whole box set from the 1990s, and we are really into that lately. It is really cool. We are just gonna drink and watch Friends and smoke pot. Life is great."

At the time, it is awesome. Then you have a kid and you are like, "What a waste!" What a waste of time up until this moment. It is the greatest club to be in. I would say that you are not a man until you are a father.

The Takeaway: Saturday Night's Changed Forever

For a man who is part of the most exclusive comedy club there is as a cast member of *SNL*, we appreciate Breuer's idea that being a dad is the greatest club to be in. We also like his take on life before and after becoming a dad. It isn't that all the things you did for enjoyment prior to becoming a dad weren't fun and awesome and memorable. They most certainly were (even the stuff you can't really remember from your "getting after it" college or post-college days). However, once you become a dad, it can provide an anchor for your future happiness. Embrace that.

What to Say Before Going to Outer Space (or Away on Business)
Scott Kelly

DADOGRAPHY

Twitter: @StationCDRKelly
Born: February 21, 1964
Kids: Samantha, Charlotte
Career: Engineer, Astronaut, US Navy Captain

If you took almost all of the awesome jobs you wanted as a kid, rolled them into one career, and let one person live that incredible life, that one person would be Scott Kelly. Kelly is a former military fighter pilot, an engineer, a retired US Navy captain, and to top it off, he was an astronaut (but not just any astronaut). He was the commander of the International Space Station, and after three expeditions, he set the record for the most days accumulated in space by a human. While in space, he regularly recorded and uploaded videos of what life is like on the ISS to *YouTube*, racking up millions of views per video and turning him into a bona fide Internet star.

After his memoir, *Endurance: My Year in Space, a Lifetime of Discovery*, debuted in late 2017, he was able to add *New York Times* bestselling author to his list of accomplishments. While in space and thinking about writing his book, Kelly told us he spent a lot of time reflecting on his life and what his two daughters were doing while he was about as far out of physical touch as any dad could be from his kids. His perspective is unique and is a good reminder to take advantage of all the time we get to spend in person with our families.

LOD: What were some of the thoughts running through your mind about fatherhood while you were 250 miles above the earth in the International Space Station?

SK: Being isolated and not being able to be there in person for your kids if you had to is something that weighed the most on me while I was in space. I was more worried about that and something happening to them than I was about my personal safety. When you have that in your mind, it does allow you to reflect on what type of dad you are and what type of dad you would like to be.

The first time that I flew into space for each of my kids' lives they were pretty young. They were too young to comprehend exactly what I was doing. The fact that my brother was also an astronaut made it the family business that the kids have always known. That is the only thing that they have ever lived. I really never had deep discussions with them about what I was going to do. Certainly, every time that you launch into space, you tell them you love them and you give them a big hug. It is not like I have ever tried to rationalize the risk that I was taking with them.

The Takeaway: The Best Goodbye Is a Simple Goodbye

When we part ways with our kids each morning, typically with us going to work while they go to school, it's easy to take for granted that you'll be seeing them at the end of the day. Your commute, however long or short, easy or traffic-filled it is, is most likely not nearly as fraught with danger and disaster as Kelly's trips into outer space. Also, you'll more often than not be home in eight to ten hours, rather than the year that Kelly spent on the ISS.

Still, whether you're a nine-to-fiver, a heavy traveler, a work-from-home guy, or you're putting your life on the line in law enforcement or the military, when you say goodbye to your kids, get back into the habit of giving them a hug and saying "I love you" like Kelly does. It's a good daily reminder for your kids that you're thinking of them and that you care for them while you both go about your business... even if your business is in zero gravity.

One Thing: Always Be Able to Talk to Each Other
Anthony Becht

DADOGRAPHY

Twitter: @Anthony_Becht
Born: August 8, 1977
Kids: 2
Career: Philanthropist, TV Analyst, NFL Player

ESPN college football analyst and former NFL veteran Anthony Becht spent twelve years in the trenches as a tight end for the New York Jets, Tampa Bay Bucs, and the (then) St. Louis Rams, among others. He's the host of the *Spittin' Fire* podcast and still works as a color man occasionally for the two teams he spent the most time with, the Jets and Bucs. Though football is his first love, he's branched out into hosting on the Home Shopping Network, working as a motivational speaker, and being an entrepreneur.

During the college football season, when he's not jumping from college campus to college campus to cover games, he's either at the beach with his family (they stayed in Tampa after he played there) or spending time with his kids.

LOD: You've had to build strong relationships with your two kids while playing a time-demanding sport with travel and several moves involved. What's worked for you?

AB: When I am looking at my daughter and my son and trying to build relationships, the one thing that is very important to us as they get older is for them to know that they can talk to me or my wife. They can tell us their problems and not be afraid that we are going to jump down their throat. There might be consequences, but they know that we will still love them.

I think that is the one thing that maybe some parents don't want to talk about. Every day, my wife and I tell our kids we love them and hug them. We tell them that they can always talk to us. Granted, they are eight and ten years old and they don't have that many major problems in their lives. That is the age where you want to let them know and feel comfortable to come to you. We have been there. There were certain things where you didn't want to reach out to your parents.

So that is the number one thing for me. It is to tell them that you love them, hug them, and let them know that they can come to you, no matter what.

The Takeaway: Open Communication and Unconditional Love

We all want our kids to feel like they can tell us anything. Our parents probably wanted the same thing. For whatever reason, far too many kids feel like they have to hide things from their parents in order to avoid being uncomfortable, enduring a punishment, or feeling judged. If we assume that because we have a good relationship with our kids they'll be open with us, we're fooling ourselves. That's not enough. We need to remind them every day that not only do we love them but we're here for them to talk (even if we won't like what they're going to tell us).

And here's a quick tip from experience: regardless of the conversation, never freak out about what you hear. Maintain a poker face throughout the conversation, and your kids will see you as someone who is calm and reliable to talk to. If you freak out, they'll freak out, and that's not good for either of you.

Part II
Talk—What to Know

Part I was all about your kids. Part II is all about you.

Let's face it: being a modern father is an all-encompassing responsibility that no longer involves "mom" things and "dad" things. Long gone are the days where dads raised their kids without ever touching a diaper. Or making school lunches. Or taking the kids to the doctor. Or putting the kids to bed.

Thankfully, people no longer think of dads who are alone with their kids as "babysitting" because "mom's busy." As society has evolved and blurred the lines between what were long-considered "mom" roles and "dad" roles in the household, we are the new breed of dad. We are the breed of dad who has a full-time job and takes the kids school-supplies shopping. We are the breed of dad who picks up the kids from school and sets up a playdate and watches them solo while mom's on a business trip. We are, in short, men on equal footing with women in the parenting department.

With that change, however, comes challenges that men from previous generations never really had to face. Issues like work/family balance weren't a "thing" because dads worked and that's what they did. Time management skills weren't so readily discussed because there was only one career in the household, and it was dad's career, and that was it. Health issues were kept private or not discussed openly because we were supposed to "man up" and deal with it.

This isn't just "old school" thinking versus "new school" thinking. This is a complete reimagining of the family dynamic. It's a generation of dads learning on the fly how to balance all of these new responsibilities that our own dads rarely dealt with. And while most dads today embrace their roles, there's no shame in admitting that it's not easy and sometimes we could use some advice and help from other dads on how to make it all work.

This section of the book is designed to help you with all of these challenges. It will discuss the strategies, tips, and tactics that dads can use in their own lives to improve everything from work/life balance to their marriage to handling serious challenges like their own health issues or even more difficult health problems with their children. You will find actionable advice with stories and plenty of lessons learned from fathers who have won championships, built *Fortune* 500 companies, started brewing empires, served in the Navy, founded major fitness brands, and yet accomplished more as fathers than they did as men.

CHAPTER 7

Embracing New Roles

"It is not the strongest or the most intelligent who will survive but those who can best manage change."
—Charles Darwin, Father of Ten

Newborn Rules: What Not to Do When You Go Back to Work
Dale Earnhardt Jr.

DADOGRAPHY

Twitter: @DaleJr
Born: October 10, 1974
Kid: Isla Rose
Career: NASCAR Legend

As a third-generation race car driver and the son of one of the most famous and successful racers of all time, Dale Earnhardt Jr. had an enormous amount of pressure on him as he began his own NAS-CAR career behind the wheel. His father, Dale Earnhardt Sr., aka the Intimidator, won seven Winston Cup championships, including a Daytona 500 win in 1998. Junior could have been forgiven for shying away from the pressure or faltering under the weight of expectations, but he did neither of those things.

Over the course of his own racing career, he won over twenty races, including two Daytona 500s (2004 and 2014), while also being voted NASCAR's most popular driver fifteen times in a row. In terms of most influential athletes of his generation, he is often listed in the same breath as luminaries like Derek Jeter, Peyton Manning, and LeBron James. When we spoke with Junior, he had just completed his autobiography, *Racing to the Finish*, and started on the next phase of his life: fatherhood.

LOD: Since you are in the thick of it in terms of becoming a new dad with an infant at home, do you have any advice for other brand-new dads or guys whose partners are due with their first child soon?

DE: You're going to be at home for a bit after your baby is born, and then life goes on and you go back to doing whatever it is you do. You're going to be doing the things at night that your wife's doing. You're going to be fixing bottles and feeding and struggling to get a good night's sleep. And then you'll have to go to work. But one thing you can't do when you get home is talk about how tired you are. Even if you had the worst day, don't walk in the door and say, "You aren't gonna believe this," because your wife doesn't care. You're wasting your time.

Nothing that happened to you that day is going to matter. It took me a while to really understand that, and I still catch myself talking to my wife about something that has stressed me out and then I realize I shouldn't be complaining about this because I don't have half the responsibility she has taking care of this little baby all day, every day. Everything everybody says about fatherhood is true. Once that baby is home, you've got to dial back what you think and focus on your wife and keeping her and your new baby healthy. You want things to go as smooth as possible since she's probably going to be doing most of the work.

The Takeaway: Let Your Mind Race, but Your Mouth Rest

When we talked to Dale Earnhardt Jr., he was smack dab in the middle of adjusting to life as a dad. His daughter was only a few months old, and we could hear the joy in his voice. He was embracing all the fun of fatherhood while also understanding the unique role of motherhood during that crazy/tired/wonderful time…and his advice is spot on. If there's ever a time in your life to be totally selfless, it's as the dad of a newborn. Do whatever you can to keep mom and baby happy. How best to do that in your own situation is up to you. It may be as simple as offering to give your wife a much-needed night away from the baby (and you) by setting up (or at least encouraging) a girls' night for her. Or it could be that you volunteer to take all the night feeding shifts for the weekend so your wife can sleep. Every situation is different, but keep an eye out for how best you can help.

Handling Tantrums and Taking Advice from Kevin Bacon
Hank Azaria

DADOGRAPHY

Twitter: @HankAzaria
Born: April 25, 1964
Kid: Hal
Career: Actor, Voice Actor, Comedian, Producer

At last count, Hank Azaria was responsible for more than twenty voices on *The Simpsons,* including Moe, Apu, Chief Wiggum, the Comic Book Guy, and a roster of rotating characters with so many different accents, tones, timbres, and styles that it's hard to believe their voices are coming from the same person. There's hardly a region or dialect that Azaria can't mimic (or make up) with his vocal wizardry, but he kept two voices in his holster for quite a long time: baby talk and toddler talk.

Azaria, who has also appeared in dozens of feature films and TV shows as an actor, didn't become a father until later in his life and, in fact, wasn't sure he wanted to have children. In the ultimate irony, he found out his wife was pregnant while filming a documentary called *Fatherhood*, which was a pet project where Azaria interviewed many of his famous friends about being a dad. He began the project as part of his effort to decide whether he should have kids or not.

Spoiler alert: he did (and he loves it) and he got some great advice along the way.

LOD: Your *Fatherhood* series is great. We agree with your take on tantrums. Can you share that and also some of the solid advice you got for how to deal with them?

HA: With tantrums, I found them very daunting. I didn't want to flip out. I didn't want to make a mistake. I also wanted to keep my own sanity. One of the main things is that you can't give in. You can't give them what they are wanting. If you do, then the lesson they learn there is that "if I flip out, I get what I want." You don't want them doing that.

You also don't want to respond to a tantrum with a tantrum. You don't want to be emotional in the face of a tantrum. You want to pick your battles. You can do certain things to head off tantrums if you know they are coming. Transitioning a kid is a big deal. Instead of just saying, "Okay, we got to go," you tell them, "We are leaving in five minutes.... Finish up what you are doing because in two minutes we got to get out of here."

Think about it. You wouldn't like it if you were told that. You were doing something and I said, "Hey, let's go." It takes a lot of practice. That's why I like to get advice from experts and other dads. It is good to get help on things like that.

Kevin Bacon, before I had a kid, he said the phases of childhood will drive you crazy. But whether you love them or hate them, they will pass. They don't say that in the books. Including the tantrum phase. They stop with the tantrums after a while.

When my son was two, he was like a cherub—he was completely angelic. The second he turned three, he became maniacal. Love it or hate it, the phase is not going to last. When you look at it that way, it helps you appreciate the good times and know that the bad times are not going to last forever.

The Takeaway: Six Degrees of Tantrum Advice from Kevin Bacon

One great, actionable piece of advice is far better than empty platitudes, and Azaria's thoughts on handling tantrums is dead on. No matter how frustrating they are (and they can be mind-blowingly infuriating), trying to stop a tantrum with a tantrum of your own won't work. Stay cool, stay calm, and be steady. It'll pass.

But hey, don't take it from us. Next time you handle your kid's meltdown like a pro and someone compliments you, just tell them Kevin Bacon gave you some tips. (And, technically, it's only four degrees: Kevin to Hank to us to you.)

Being an Accidental Parent
Thomas Lennon

DADOGRAPHY

Twitter: @ThomasLennon
Born: August 9, 1970
Kid: Oliver
Career: Actor, Voice Actor, Comedian, Producer

There are two kinds of people who came of age in the 1990s. Those who worshipped MTV's sketch comedy show *The State*, and everyone else. If you're in the former category, like we are, and you can quote Doug's lines and Louie's catch phrases and Barry and Levon's pudding references, then you know who Thomas Lennon is (he's Barry). Also, he was one-half of the famous make-out scene with Paul Rudd in *I Love You, Man*.

Lennon has been in a host of other movies and TV shows, including a starring role on Comedy Central's *Reno 911!*, where he played Lieutenant Jim Dangle with his iconic, skin-tight, thigh-high shorts. The shorts, in fact, are a go-to punch line for Lennon when he talks about why he became a father older than expected. We'll let him explain.

LOD: You didn't become a father until later in your life, and for a while you thought you might not become one. What advice do you have for older dads with young kids, and what went through your mind when you found out your wife was pregnant?

TL: The first thing that I thought was she must be kidding. This can't be possible. I had been wearing those Lieutenant Dangle shorts for six years at that point. I thought I must have done permanent damage to myself. This can't be so. We had tried for a long time. Jenny is a little bit older than me. It didn't seem like it was working out. We became accidental parents. It was a total surprise for us.

Oliver was born and they handed him to me. I thought, "What happens now? What should I do?" I didn't know what to do. I was standing there. Jenny had a C-section so she had to go into recovery for a little bit. I was completely alone with Oliver. It was a very strange feeling.

The thing that I found out about parenting is that 50 percent of what people tell you is not true. It is true for them. They are just sharing their experience. They are not really telling truths about parenting. It changes all the time.

The one thing that I did find surprising is that almost everything that you need to know about being a dad will reveal itself to you when you need it. Again, this could be not true for everyone, but I am telling you my experience. I got a stack of books on parenting that we never got through. Parenting is like that great quote that "everyone has a plan until they get punched in the face." Parenting is exactly that. You have so many plans and then, bam!

The Takeaway: Entering "the State" of Fatherhood Is Different for Everyone

Whether you become a dad at twenty-five or thirty-five or forty-five years old, the first time you hold your child alone, you will think the exact same thing as Lennon: "What do I do now?" The beautiful thing is that you'll quickly figure it out. Everyone does.

We really like Lennon's quotes about unread parenting books and having "parenting" plans. You never know what will work until you try something with your own kid because the relationship you have with your children is totally unique. Embrace that fact and don't worry about what worked for other people. Just worry about what works for you.

What to Text New Dads

Brad Stevens

DADOGRAPHY

Twitter: @BCCoachStevens
Born: October 22, 1976
Kids: Brady, Kinsley
Career: NBA Basketball Head Coach

If Gordon Hayward's last-second, half-court shot at the end of the 2010 NCAA tournament finals against Duke had been about three inches lower off the glass, Butler University would have won its first NCAA championship and the team's head coach, Brad Stevens, would already have one title on his resume.

Cut to eight years later, and Hayward and Stevens have reunited on the Boston Celtics. Stevens is the head coach and Hayward one of the team's stars (along with Kyrie Irving, Jayson Tatum, and Jaylen Brown). When Celtics General Manager Danny Ainge plucked Stevens from his job in the Horizon League, he went from being the second-youngest coach in Division I basketball to becoming the youngest coach in the National Basketball Association. No matter. In his second season with Boston, he made the playoffs and he has since been to the Eastern Conference Finals twice.

He is the father of two and told us that there are plenty of similarities between being a head coach and a father. He uses the same strategies with both jobs, but nothing beats being a dad. "Oh man, being a father is the greatest," he told us. "To have the chance to celebrate the birth of your own child and watch them grow and develop and learn and experience new things has been the ultimate blessing. I have a number of players, both college and pro, that have had kids in the last few years. I always text them the exact same thing when I get the introductory text to their newborn. It is: 'There is nothing better.'"

LOD: What are some of the similarities between coaching and fatherhood that you've noticed?

BS: Both responsibilities are very important. You want to put your signature on this job. You want to do the very best you can. You want the people you are working with to feel like you are invested in them and that you are putting a lot of time and thought into them. You want to do that with your own children. You want them to know that you are doing everything you can to help them have a great next day and that you are there to support their passions and help them find out what they like to do. You try to give them any advice here or there that might help put them into a position to enjoy and experience life even more. My kids are young, so the challenges they face are much different than what twenty-two-year-olds face, but nonetheless you feel a great amount of responsibility doing both.

The Takeaway: Send a Championship-Level Congratulatory Text

As a man who is responsible for his own young kids, as well as the young men he's coached, Coach Stevens's comparison between fatherhood and coaching provides valuable advice for parents with kids of all ages—specifically the idea of letting your kids know that you're invested in them. Yes, we love our kids, but in terms of time, energy, and emotion, "invest" is probably the best way to describe our all-out effort to raise our kids. A great way to show this is to schedule a few trips or attend some talks with your kids on topics that only they care about. For instance, you may have no interest in their favorite hobby, but make a few *Google* searches about festivals or conferences about that hobby and surprise your kid with tickets.

And, the next time a buddy or colleague has a kid, don't worry about what to write. Just steal Coach Stevens's line and text: "Congratulations! There's nothing better!"

Take One Part of Your Kids' Daily Schedule and Make It Your Priority
Ben Falcone

DADOGRAPHY

Twitter: @BenFalcone
Born: August 25, 1973
Kids: Georgette, Vivian
Career: Comedian, Actor, Filmmaker, Author

Not only is actor-writer-director Ben Falcone a comedian at heart, he is married to one of the most successful female comedians of all time, Melissa McCarthy. The first couple of comedy (we just made that up) have joined forces on several films that they cowrote (and that Falcone directed), including *Tammy*, *The Boss*, and *Superintelligence*. Off camera, they have also produced two daughters.

When we talked to Falcone, it was on the heels of the release of his first book, *Being a Dad Is Weird: Lessons in Fatherhood from My Family to Yours*. The book explores Falcone's relationship with his father, who had a larger-than-life personality, along with his own thoughts on fatherhood and things that other parents do that often annoy him (like blocking his view to film an entire dance recital with their phones).

LOD: With you and your wife often collaborating on the same projects and with the notoriously long hours on a film set, how do you manage your schedule so you build in time with your kids as they get older?

BF: I tell people that the work can go on and on, so it's time to go. I am out and you should be out. Go home. Everyone go home and be with your family. Sometimes if I have a lot of work going on, I will get home and put the kids to bed, then I will finish work when the kids go to bed. That is okay. I just definitely need that time with them.

I personally can't just try and finish everything up and then realize I didn't see my kids all day. I take them to school every day. They have been razzing me that I don't pick them up every day. I tell them that I am doing pretty good. They tell me that other parents pick their kids up every day. Still, Melissa and I put family first. Whenever we do a project and have to travel, we take the whole family with us. We travel as a little weird group. We call ourselves a little circus.

The Takeaway: Regardless of Your Schedule, Create One Daily Habit with Your Kids

Falcone has decided he will drive his kids to school every day. This gives him time to talk with them, have fun with them, and stay up to date on what's going on in their lives. We all have responsibilities that pull us away from our families, and too often we forget to build time with our kids into our day. Whether you have breakfast together, pick up your kids, find time for a book or puzzle, or even take a walk after dinner (or FaceTime if you travel), letting your kids know that no matter what, there is one part of your day that is devoted to them is extremely important.

The Beauty of Savoring Moments
Mark Cuban

DADOGRAPHY

Twitter: @MCuban
Born: July 31, 1958
Kids: Alexa, Alyssa, Jake
Career: Entrepreneur, Businessman, Investor, NBA Owner

To pro basketball fans, Mark Cuban has been the maverick owner of the Dallas Mavericks since 2000 and a hero in Dallas–Fort Worth thanks to their 2011 national championship (the franchise's first). To entrepreneurs and business junkies, Cuban is arguably the most popular "shark" on ABC's hit series *Shark Tank* as well as the guy who sold Broadcast.com to *Yahoo!* in 1999 for $5.9 billion in stock. And to those who follow the modern start-up scene, Cuban is nearly omnipresent, investing in companies not only on *Shark Tank* but also across the software, entertainment, social media, and analytics industries.

Admittedly, he says that beyond his three kids having fun at Mavericks' games, they could care less about his TV hosting or his business savvy and that all the publicity surrounding him and the media attention is just a distraction. They simply see him as Dad. And that's more than enough to make him go from ruthless shark to harmless teddy bear.

LOD: With the number of companies you're in charge of and the commitments you have through *Shark Tank*, how do you balance your time between business and fatherhood?

MC: I'm fortunate. I put business first before I got married. I managed to be successful beyond my wildest dreams, which let me put family first once I got married and had kids. So now I schedule around my kids as much as possible. I can't make all their games, but I make most. The difference is the most important words in my life used to be "you have a deal" or "yes" to a deal. Now my heart melts every time my kids tell me they love me or just call me Dad. It's crazy how much I just want to lock those moments in a time capsule and hold on to them forever. My priorities are dramatically different now.

The Takeaway: Be a Shark about Your Time with Your Family

It doesn't matter if you have one job or three, if you're an hourly employee or you run your own company—when it comes to spending time with your kids, you've got to have your priorities in order. You also have to make sure you stay in the moment. It's easy to get used to your kids saying "I love you" and running up to hug you after school or when you get home from work, but the days of them being "little" will fly by, and like Cuban, you'll want to lock those moments in a mental time capsule forever. Once you're a dad, take Cuban's advice and in addition to focusing on the "highs" you get from wins at work, enjoy the wins at home too.

What Unconditional Love Is Like

Adam Savage

DADOGRAPHY

Twitter: @DontTryThis
Born: July 15, 1967
Kids: Addison, Riley
Career: Special Effects Designer, Actor, Educator, TV Host

In many ways, the name of Adam Savage's former show, *Myth-Busters*, has become so synonymous with cool experiments that it's used much like Q-tips for ear swabs or Kleenex for tissues. Anytime someone discusses blowing something up or launching something into the air or testing out something they saw in a movie, they say they're going to do some mythbusting, even if no myth is actually being busted. The Discovery Channel show, which ran for ten years with the original hosts, Savage and his on-screen partner/foil Jamie Hyneman (both now producers on the new version), tapped into something visceral and exciting every time they put a movie trope (cars blowing up when they're shot) or a cliché (float like a lead balloon) to the test on screen.

In addition to the show, Savage is a special effects designer for some of Hollywood's biggest movies, including several in the Star Wars series. He's also an accomplished sculptor, a dedicated educator, and a father to twin boys he affectionately calls Thing One and Thing Two. Considering his background, it is no surprise that when Savage found out he was going to become a father, he stole a few tactics from his science background to come to grips with his new role.

LOD: When it comes to science, you get to test theories over and over and study the outcome. With kids, you get one shot to do as well as you can. What did you apply from your career to fatherhood?

AS: Back before [the twins] were born, I was doing what everyone does when they are getting ready to have kids. I was thinking, "How am I going to screw this up?" I had this singular thought. I approached it scientifically, actually. I said, "What is the worst-case scenario? What is the worst thing that can happen to people when they are raised wrong? What is the single missing thing?"

To me, people are raised in all types of egregious conditions: emotional, physical, etc. In my experience with the friends that I have made over the years with their stories both good and bad, the one thing that really screws you up is not feeling like you were loved by one or both of your parents. That is one of the most difficult things to recover from. I know people who have recovered from that and found their own love for themselves. That is one of the hardest things to really recover from. People who can't love their kids or let their kids know that they are loved have no business having children.

I knew that no matter what else I would screw up, they would never doubt for a second that I loved them. That has absolutely been the case. Like I said, raising kids is a terrifying ordeal and it is also amazing. There are many points where you beat yourself up for feeling like you were doing it wrong. When that happens, I remind myself that my kids feel completely loved by me and by all the adults in their life.

The Takeaway: Using Occam's Razor As a Parenting Strategy

Occam's Razor is a scientific principle that simply states that when comparing solutions to a problem, the simplest explanation tends to be the right one. Like Savage, it's so easy for dads (especially new dads) to get caught up in all the different strategies people offer for raising kids. Don't overcomplicate it. Rather than try to do everything right, we like his approach: just get one thing right. Make sure your kids know you love them, no matter what. The rest will take care of itself.

Every Day of Fatherhood Is Brand New

Sterling K. Brown

DADOGRAPHY

Twitter: @SterlingKBrown
Born: April 5, 1976
Kids: Andrew, Amaré
Career: Actor

Before Sterling K. Brown became "the guy" on TV with Emmy wins for his portrayal of Christopher Darden in *The People v. O.J. Simpson: American Crime Story* and his life-altering role as Randall Pearson on NBC's mega-hit show *This Is Us*, Brown was "that guy" in dozens of plays and had singular or recurring roles on other hit TV series like *ER*, *NYPD Blue*, *Alias*, *Supernatural*, and many, many more.

Brown attended Stanford University and got his MFA from New York University, and the only thing he's wanted longer than to be a successful actor is to be a parent. He lost his father when he was only ten years old and told us that he has a wealth of emotion inside of him regarding his dad and his presence and lack of presence in his life. "I had some of the best ten years of love that I could have ever experienced," he said of his dad. "It was unfiltered. It was pure. It was unconditional."

With two children of his own, Brown is now determined to provide the same feeling of unfiltered and unconditional love to his boys.

LOD: You're currently playing one of the most popular, beloved dads on TV as Randall Pearson on *This Is Us*. How much of your

own experiences from being a dad have you pulled into the role, and what advice do you have for other dads out there in their day-to-day lives?

SB: I wanted to be a dad since I was about eighteen or nineteen years old. I knew I wasn't ready to be a dad, but I wanted it very much. Sometimes I would tell my friends while I was getting my undergrad at Stanford that I would get graduate-student housing and carry my kid with me to all my classes. I would find a way to make it work. My friends would say, "Why don't you try getting a dog first? [He laughs.] Let's see how that works and see if you can extrapolate from there."

It was something that always felt right for me. For me to fully realize myself as a person meant becoming a father. It just felt like the natural evolution of things. When my wife became pregnant with Andrew, my first son, I just started crying. I can remember seeing the first ultrasound. I was thinking that the miracle is happening.

The advice that I would give is the advice that I always get from my mom. It is to enjoy every minute. Especially as a new dad. Try to be as present as possible because day to day, they become brand new. They discover something new. Their first laugh is such a priceless moment. Just hearing what makes your kid giggle will give you so much joy. Enjoy all of it.

Also knowing that in the beginning, you will be exhausted, but remember this too shall pass. While it may seem like an eternity in that moment, it is not. Maintain your cool. Take a deep breath and love your child through whatever they are going through.

The Takeaway: Take In the Daily Discoveries

We hear many people give the advice to "enjoy every moment" of fatherhood, and that advice isn't wrong, and the cliché that time goes by quickly with kids isn't wrong either. Perhaps it's the packaging of the advice that makes us skip over it sometimes. Nobody can really enjoy every moment, especially in the beginning on no sleep and with no schedule. Try approaching each day with the thought that you're going to discover something different about your child, as Brown says. You'll find energy and gratitude in those daily discoveries.

Why Happiness Matters More Than Anything
Chris Long

DADOGRAPHY

Twitter: @JOEL9ONE
Born: March 28, 1985
Kid: Waylon
Career: NFL Player, Philanthropist

Chris Long the philanthropist saves lives. Full stop. Following a trip to climb Mt. Kilimanjaro in 2013, he became infatuated with the people of Tanzania, admiring them for their energy and culture. He also became worried. Due to a lack of clean water, many Tanzanians, particularly children, were suffering from a variety of medical issues and maladies that could be alleviated with clean drinking water. After being educated about the crisis and learning about ways to end the suffering, Long started Waterboys.org, an organization dedicated to not only drilling wells in East Africa but also bringing much-needed educational and health resources to the area. Nearly a dozen other professional athletes have now signed on as "water boys" to help the cause.

Oh, that's right, we haven't mentioned it yet: Chris Long is a four-time NFL Pro Bowler and two-time Super Bowl champion. His father is Pro Football Hall of Famer and broadcaster Howie Long and his brother Kyle also plays in the league.

Along with his trip to Tanzania, the other life-changing moment that occurred in Long's life was a little closer to home: he became a dad.

LOD: With your dad playing in the NFL, football was in your blood. You were also a sociology major at the University of Virginia, so you were prepared for your professional and philanthropic careers. How has fatherhood affected you and what's the most important aspect of parenting to you?

CL: I always thought that I was somebody whose professional life was most important—what I wanted to accomplish on the field, off the field, all of those things. I wanted to wait and wait to have kids. I was thirty-one when I had my son, but I wish that I had done it sooner. Conquer your fears. Just trust the miracle that is fatherhood. It is going to speak to you in a way that nothing ever has.

Happiness and self-worth are most important. We will figure out what his personality is, but I think every kid should be happy and feel like they are worth a lot. I know that I always felt that way growing up in my household. It was a household full of love. I just hope that my son looks at me as a friend and someone that he can receive guidance from. It is not a relationship where he is afraid of his dad or worrying if he is going to be in trouble. Hopefully, we can create a home where he is happy and he knows that he is worth a lot. He knows right from wrong, but the most important thing to me is that he is a happy kid. Having a child at the right time is going to be the best decision you will ever make.

The Takeaway: Never Underestimate Happiness

Long, who clearly has the compassionate gene, is keen to recognize how crucial it is for children to feel that they are loved and valued.

When kids are young, instilling that sense of self-worth largely comes from parents. Taking conscious steps to make sure you're putting that at the forefront of whatever your parenting strategy is will pay dividends; not only for you but for your child's happiness as well. The simplest way to do this is to get into the habit of asking their opinions about things. As parents, we often fall into the trap of planning and taking care of everything and then asking our kids to go along for the ride. Moving forward, when situations come up that involve your children, remember to sit down and ask their opinion on the topic (and even better, follow their advice once in a while).

CHAPTER 8

Managing Priorities

"The key is not to prioritize what's on your schedule,
but to schedule your priorities."
—Stephen Covey, Father of Nine (Grandfather of Fifty-Two)

How to Handle Stress
Henry Winkler

DADOGRAPHY

Twitter: @HWinkler4Real
Born: October 30, 1945
Kids: Max, Zoe
Career: Actor, Author, Producer, Writer

Forty-five years after Henry Winkler introduced the world to "The Fonz" on the iconic show *Happy Days*, he took home his first Emmy Award in the Outstanding Supporting Actor category for his role as Gene Cousineau on HBO's *Barry*. Throughout his nearly five-decade career, Winkler appeared in a wide variety of movies, including *The Waterboy* and *Scream*. In addition to his roles on screen, he has built a reputation as one of the nicest guys in Hollywood.

What many Winkler fans don't know is that he grew up with dyslexia and had a very hard time overcoming his learning disability. Specifically, he had a difficult time learning to read. Recognizing that there were thousands of kids growing up with the same challenges, Winkler created the children's literary series Henry Zipzer: The World's Greatest Underachiever, about a bright boy who overcomes learning issues. Winkler has always been drawn to work with kids and has two (now grown-up) children.

LOD: During the early part of your career on *Happy Days*, you were one of the biggest stars on TV and you also had little kids. What were some of the challenges?

HW: One of the challenges was to make sure that the children were kept out of the public eye. Another challenge was to make sure that our home life was as normal and consistent as possible. And a third major challenge was to make sure that the children were not spoiled. I think boundaries are unbelievably important to help a child to feel secure. Chores is another concept that was important to me. Our children were great negotiators—I did their chores.

LOD: When you were dealing with craziness on set and then craziness at home with young kids, how did you relieve stress?

HW: Walk out of the room. Take a swim. Watch TV. Leave the house. Explain very clearly to the children that I was in a bad mood and they could either leave me alone or suffer the gorilla that was about to jump out of my body.

The Takeaway: Amidst Kid Chaos, Be Like The Fonz and Be Cool

When the word *priorities* comes up, many of us immediately default to thinking about our schedule and how we manage our time. However, another priority that is equally as important is your mental well-being. There are plenty of times—especially when your kids are little, you're tired, and you've had a long day—that the children drive you nuts and you just want to lose it and scream your head off. Don't. Instead, take Winkler's advice and find ways to disengage to get your head right. Rather than your kids watching you lose your cool and looking like a maniac, tell them you need to take a walk, take a few deep breaths, or find your own way to decompress.

Kids Must Be the Priority
Titus O'Neil

DADOGRAPHY

Twitter: @TitusONeilWWE
Born: April 29, 1977
Kids: Titus, Thaddeus
Career: WWE Wrestler, Entertainer

Even before Titus O'Neil made a name for himself in the bright lights of the WWE, he made a name for himself in The Swamp at Gainesville, playing college football for the University of Florida Gators and legendary coach Steve Spurrier. After injuring his knee in training camp with the Jacksonville Jaguars, he bounced around the Arena League before chasing his dream of becoming a pro wrestler by participating in the second season of *WWE NXT*. In a short period of time, he became a WWE Tag Team Champion with Darren Young as part of the Prime Time Players.

Aside from challenges on the field and in the ring, one of the biggest obstacles O'Neil has had to overcome in his life was growing up without a father. To counter that, he has worked with the Ad Council on its "Take Time to Be a Dad Today" campaign, and as a father of two boys, O'Neil makes sure to cherish every moment he has with his sons.

LOD: WWE stars notoriously have the most hectic work schedules imaginable. What is your strategy to spend as much time with your kids as you can?

TO: I just make it a priority. I don't believe anybody should say that they are too busy to hang out with their kids. I think it is maybe more dear to me just because I didn't grow up with a father. I didn't grow up with a male figure in our home. So it was always important to me when I became a father to have my kids never feel the way I did or have the issues that I dealt with when I was a kid.

Although my schedule is very hectic, I still keep in contact with my kids when I am on the road. They both have iPads so we FaceTime together. They call me regularly to let me know how their day went. They call me pretty much every night. When I am home, I try to structure everything to be able to spend as much time as I possibly can. That is one of the main reasons that I work out at five in the morning. I can get up, go work out, and then take them to school.

I run all the errands while they are at school so when they get out of school I can be completely devoted to what they have to do. We help with their homework and go to their sports practices. I always try and be one of the coaches. It is actually pretty cool for them and me. A lot of their teammates are WWE fans, so it is always a great opportunity to bring their team together faster.

The Takeaway: All Time Is Quality Time

When Titus O'Neil told us that he didn't believe anybody should say they are too busy to hang out with their kids, all we could do is nod our heads in agreement. And having grown up without a father, his perspective on the matter is all the more impactful. Whether you have to wake up at 5 a.m. to work out or get work in, you should analyze your schedule, find out what you can get done either early in the morning or late at night, and use the time you've freed up during the day to devote to your kids. No excuses.

How to Set Boundaries and Lead by Example
Kevin Cleary

> **DADOGRAPHY**
>
> Twitter: @KevinClearyCEO
> Kids: 3
> Career: Entrepreneur, CEO

As we quickly learned, Kevin Cleary, CEO of Clif Bar, is serious about how he structures his company and his life. On the company front, Clif Bar is guided by what they call their Five Aspirations, which are: sustaining their business, their brands, their people, their community, and their planet. On the personal side, Cleary walks the walk on several fronts. He is committed to the health of employees, and he makes sure they regularly see him going for bike rides and exercising on company time (Clif Bar actually pays people to exercise!). He is an avid cycler and runner and has completed several half marathons while also competing on NBC's popular show *American Ninja Warrior*.

In addition to fitness, he is committed to his employees' overall well-being, which includes letting them set their priorities so they can engage fully in their work and home life. Here, too, he sets the tone, leading by example. When he coaches his sons' teams, he often ducks out of the office early to make practice or a game and lets it be known it's okay if others do the same as long as the work is getting done.

As a father of three, Cleary shuns the term *work/life balance*. He says it's all just life. We'll let him explain.

LOD: You have a unique perspective on the fairly new buzzword term of *work/life balance*. Can you share your thoughts?

KC: I have listened to a couple of talks lately about work/life balance and we've got to throw that out of the window. That whole concept of people somehow managing a balance sheet of life and how to do it just doesn't exist. With the iPhone and technology today, life is just life. It is just all life.

So I think the question we need to be asking is "How do we stay whole?" A lot of the things we do here at the company are about staying whole. We pay people to work out. We pay people to do community service. It is a minimum of twenty hours a year, but there is no cap on how many hours that they can contribute. It is about staying connected to the things that you love. We have on-site childcare here. You will see kids coming in and out either for lunch or just during the morning or afternoon.

It is all about trying to keep people whole. I believe that when people are whole, they are at their best. I will take seven hours of pure productivity over ten hours of drudgery any day of the week. We have high engagement here. People are committed to the purpose of the company and doing right by those five aspirations. So we get a lot of passion from the organization.

I want people to stay whole. For me it is all about living the life through the company. So I will go for a bike ride on Fridays. Sometimes I am working on Sundays. Sometimes I am cutting out early because I am coaching my sons' baseball team. There were a lot of times that I would leave at three-thirty or four to go coach my sons' team to stay connected with them. That is just important for us to think about how we stay whole, how we live our lives through work, and how it becomes seamless so it doesn't become a separate thing, like my work life and my life life.

The Takeaway: There Is No Work/Life Balance, There's Just Life

All we can say about Cleary's thoughts on work/life balance is… yes. Yes, to all of it. Life is too short to miss important events in our kids' lives or to not coach because of an outdated, antiquated notion that you must be at your desk until 5:30 or 6 p.m. every day. Of course, there are certain jobs where flexibility is not an option, but for many in the business world, the old nine-to-five mantra seems wildly outdated considering how often we're asked to be plugged in and how much larger our responsibilities are on the home front.

While many don't have a choice in this matter, more and more employees are negotiating flexible hours and work-from-home days prior to taking a job or at certain points in their employment. If you want to try this with your boss, make sure you point to what Cleary is doing at Clif Bar as an example of where it is successful for both the business and the employee.

Learning to Really Listen and Pay Attention to What Your Kids Are Saying

Bill Engvall

DADOGRAPHY

Twitter: @BillEngvall
Born: July 27, 1957
Kids: Emily, Travis
Career: Comedian, Actor

Bill Engvall's highly successful comedy career began with a lot of beer and a dare. At the time, Engvall was a DJ at a nightclub in Dallas and while watching an amateur stand-up night one of his buddies goaded him on stage. "A couple rounds of liquid courage went through us and I wanted to see what it was like," Engvall told us. "The lady who owned the club came up to me and said that she heard that I am pretty funny. By that time I was a little lit. I said, 'You heard right.' She said, 'Let's get you up on stage.' I was like, 'Why not?'"

Cut to a few years later and Engvall won the American Comedy Award for Funniest Male Stand-Up Comic. Soon, he found himself on TV shows like *Delta*, *The Jeff Foxworthy Show*, and *Designing Women*. Later, he joined best buddy Foxworthy on the Blue Collar Comedy Tour and had his own show on TBS called *The Bill Engvall Show*.

His two children, Emily and Travis (both now college graduates), provided plenty of fodder for this comedic father over the years. As his star rose, he found himself making much more of an effort to give his kids a childhood free from the traps other children of successful parents fall into.

LOD: Your family has always been a part of your act, but in real life, your career and touring would occasionally take you on the

road. You're also one of the more recognizable comedians working today. Did you come up with any strategies over the years to keep your kids grounded and to maximize your time at home?

BE: When I am at home, I try to keep a normal life as much as possible. Every once in a while, we would use the limos and all of that. For the most part, when we went on trips we were flying Southwest. We weren't flying first class. I wanted them to know that this isn't real. This is all going to go away at some point. I don't want them thinking that this is the way life is. Gail [his wife] and I tried to do a lot of keeping our kids' lives normal. They played Little League or swimming or whatever they decided to do as a hobby. We backed it full on. I wanted them to have friends. You see that some kids of actors are going to have such a messed-up life. This is not what life is. This is a wonderful sidetrack of life.

The one thing that I have learned over the years is if you listen to what your kids are saying, they will tell you what is going on in their lives. If you say, "What is going on with you?" they are not going to tell you. Just listen to them. Sometimes we as parents just kind of become background noise. It is important to listen to what they are saying. You can head off a lot of bad things before it becomes a problem. You can also find out the good stuff that is going on in their lives.

The Takeaway: Open Your Ears

Raise your hand if you've done the whole "How was school?" "Good." "Everything okay?" "Fine." question-and-answer routine with your kids at the end of the day only to have them go off and do their own thing while you go off and do yours. Instead of repeating that song and dance on a regular basis, try to ask very specific questions and simply listen to their answers. Or, better yet, open up the conversation by telling them about the important things that happened in your day, then simply listen as they return the favor. If you go through the motions of a conversation, they will too.

Take Time for Yourself
Jesse Itzler

DADOGRAPHY

Twitter: @The100Mileman
Born: August 22, 1968
Kids: Lazer, Charlie, Lincoln, Tepper
Career: Entrepreneur, Author, Rapper

Ever hear of Marquis Jet? Jesse Itzler was a cofounder. How about the coconut water that started it all, Zico? Itzler was a founding partner. And have you ever seen the Emmy Award–winning "I Love This Game" music campaign for the National Basketball Association? He produced that. His book *Living with a SEAL: 31 Days Training with the Toughest Man on the Planet* was also a *New York Times* bestseller. Oh, and he used to be a rapper on MTV. And he's run ultramarathons.

To say Itzler has a diverse set of interests would actually be unfair to the word *diverse*. Itzler's passions run the gamut from fitness to business, music, and publishing. Amazingly, he is also the father of four kids (and didn't have his first child until he was forty). The obvious question is: how? How do you accomplish all of these things while raising four kids, maintaining your sanity, and giving your wife the time she needs to manage her own multimillion-dollar business (his wife is Sara Blakely, founder of Spanx). Turns out, the answer is pretty simple.

You just need a plan.

LOD: Your list of accomplishments and responsibilities seemingly goes on forever. How do you prioritize your life, your family, and your goals to make it all work?

JI: It starts with me. I make sure that I take a couple hours during the day for myself. I call it the three-hour rule. Throughout the course of the day I allocate three hours where I can do things that I like or want to do. That could be go for a run or sit on the couch and do nothing. I don't want to have any resentment toward me and my family or my wife or work for taking away the things that I love to do. That is the starting point for me. I actually make sure that I do stuff during the day that I enjoy. I don't feel guilty when I am not doing something with my family. When I am with my family I am not having any sort of resentment of the fact that they have taken away time from the things that I like to do. So it starts with me.

My day starts off really early. It starts around five o'clock usually, when one of my four kids gets up. That process during the school year is getting them ready for school, dropping them off, and then coming home and starting my day. We have a system that works for us on what Sara's role is and what my role is and where we come together as a family. We are constantly evaluating it and seeing what is working and what is not working.

The Takeaway: Steal Itzler's Time-for-Yourself Rule

Blocking off three hours a day for yourself may not be in the cards for you if you don't work from home or run your own business, but blocking off a set amount of time, every single day, to do what you enjoy, can have a dramatic effect on your well-being and overall happiness. Far too often as dads, we continually push off doing things that make us happy and replace those things with family responsibilities. If you don't make a conscious effort to put yourself first, days, weeks, and months pass without you doing something for you. Taking time for yourself will allow you to relieve stress, nurture your passions, and replenish your energy and patience levels—all of which will make you a better dad.

The Art of Being Home
Ken Jeong

DADOGRAPHY

Twitter: @KenJeong
Born: July 13, 1969
Kids: Zooey, Alexa
Career: Doctor, Actor, Comedian

"Physician-turned-actor/comedian" is not a phrase that is typically written to describe someone's career path, but for Ken Jeong, it's spot on. Jeong graduated from Duke University, earned his MD at the University of North Carolina, Chapel Hill, and then completed his residency in internal medicine at Ochsner Medical Center in New Orleans...all while working on his stand-up career.

After winning the Big Easy Laff Off competition in 1995, Jeong moved to Los Angeles, where he continued to work on his comedy career while moonlighting (or perhaps sunlighting?) as a physician at Kaiser Permanente at Woodland Hills Medical Center. When not seeing patients, he appeared regularly on stage at the Laugh Factory and The Improv, while getting bit parts in shows like *Curb Your Enthusiasm* and *The Office*. His breakout role in *The Hangover* launched Jeong into the comedy stratosphere (and allowed him to leave his stethoscope behind forever). What followed was a starring role in the hit show *Community* and then his own show, *Dr. Ken*.

While managing a medical career and a comedy career at the same time was certainly a unique challenge, managing work life and family life is something we all deal with. Jeong is the father of two daughters and has a simple strategy for fatherhood.

LOD: You went from juggling a medical career with comedy to juggling a comedy and acting career with family. How much do you enjoy fatherhood and how do you plan your busy day so you can spend time with your wife and kids?

KJ: Being a dad is the best thing in the world. You live for your wife and kids. It just sets your priorities in life. It is everything that every dad tells you. It sounds cliché. It sounds redundant, but it is 100-percent true. It changes your goals in life. It changes your priorities. You are more focused. I think it has actually helped my life and my career. You basically determine what is important in your life and what is not.

All I do is work on the show and then be at home. I think people will be surprised by how simple my lifestyle is. I work really hard and then I am at home and I rest really hard. I think that has kind of helped keep me afloat. If I can get home by eight and put my kids to bed, I am happy. I feel like I have gotten away with something. After all, I have my own show; I get to work in Hollywood on my own project. If I can still make it back home by eight to put the kids in bed, then wow, I am having my cake and eating it too. Then I get to hang out with my wife for the rest of the night. That is my dream. That is all I really wanted.

The Takeaway: Define Your Own Dream Day

What we really liked about talking to Jeong is that he clearly defined what a great day is for him and he has built his life around achieving that. For him, it's working on a project he loves (in his case, his own TV show) and then getting home in time to put his kids to bed and be with his wife. Take some time to think about what your dream day would look like (the realistic version) and set out to make it happen. After all, if you don't define what it is, how will you ever achieve it?

Why It's Critical to Guard Your Time
Jim Koch

DADOGRAPHY

Twitter: @SamuelAdamsBeer
Born: May 27, 1949
Kids: 4
Career: Entrepreneur

Starting in the 1800s, the men of the Koch family were brewmasters, specializing in the family recipe known as Louis Koch Lager. Unfortunately, by the mid-twentieth century, the market for American-made beer dwindled so low that Jim Koch's dad put the recipe in his attic, hung up his hops, and changed careers. Jim Koch, however, believed in that recipe, and after a thirty-five-year lull of nobody brewing the family lager, he sensed that the time had come to bring it back in the early 1980s.

After famously experimenting with the recipe in his kitchen and then going bar door to bar door to sell the updated version (a beer he called Samuel Adams), he began to officially rebuild the family business in 1985. Bottle by bottle and barrel by barrel, Koch grew his brewing empire into what it is today: one of America's best success stories and a beer label recognized worldwide.

Koch, a father of four, admits that the hours required to put his stamp on the beer industry often made his family life difficult, but through his honesty comes some great tips on how to make things work if you're starting your own business.

LOD: You have a legendary work ethic and an obsessive drive to promote Sam Adams and all of its different varieties. How did

that affect your ability to raise your kids and how do you think you handled balancing your job and family?

JK: Poorly, much of the time. Starting and growing a business can be an eighty-hour-a-week commitment. In the early years of Sam Adams, when my two oldest kids were little, I didn't travel as much. My time with them was sacred, and I could usually build work around that. But then, when the company took off, that became more difficult. When I remarried and had two more children, I became far more protective of my time with the girls, but by then, I was traveling much of every month. We take family vacations and spend good chunks of time together in the summer. But, it's a struggle, and anyone who tells you it isn't is lying.

Childhood is not infinite. Guard your family time. It's way more finite than you realize. Having raised four children, I realized that by the time your child is twelve, you will have already spent 75 percent of the time you will ever spend together. When they're twelve, you're already on the last 25 percent of your time with them. Treasure it. Take them to work with you sometimes. It's good for them to see what the other piece of your life is like.

The Takeaway: Treat Time with Your Kids As Sacred Time

Leave it to a tremendously successful entrepreneur to come up with a formula for how much time we'll spend with our kids by a certain age. But we're very glad he did. The percentage that he put in our heads is striking. By the time kids are age twelve, you will have spent 75 percent of the time you will ever spend with your kids being home. It's a scary and humbling number, and it is an important one to keep in mind. Every day that percentage moves toward less and less time with your kids. Protect that time. Guard that time. Spend it wisely.

You Need to Fight for Family Time
Kevin Millar

DADOGRAPHY

Twitter: @KMillar15
Born: September 24, 1971
Kids: Kanyon, Kashten, Kiley, Karis
Career: MLB Player, TV Host

After four years playing for the Florida Marlins from 1998 to 2002, Kevin Millar was on his way to play for the Chunichi Dragons of the Japanese Central League when the Boston Red Sox interrupted the deal and signed him. Millar quickly became a locker-room and fan favorite, helping to spark the American League Championship Series run the Red Sox made in 2003 and then the magical 2004 season, which included coming back from being down 0-3 to the New York Yankees in a seven-game series to win the American League Championship, and then the World Series a week later. He'd go on to play for the Baltimore Orioles, Toronto Blue Jays, and Chicago Cubs before retiring in 2010.

Millar is currently the host of *Intentional Talk* on the MLB Network and proudly gets to spend much more time with his four kids now than he did when they were little during his playing days.

LOD: Everyone knows you as a fun-loving guy. What are some of the key things that you prioritize and embrace in your role as "dad"?

KM: What I always tell people is that having a child is responsibility. It is not sticking an iPad in his face for eight hours. You've got to play. It is work. It is fun work, but it is a job. There are times where you want to put your feet up. You are pulling your hair out and you haven't talked to your wife for a week. Yet you enjoy those times because it goes so fast. I want my kids to remember that I am always loving and that daddy needs a kiss before I drop you off at school or you are not leaving. I want them to know love. When we drop them off at school, I always say you give daddy kisses, no matter what. To this day when I see my dad, I hug him and give him a kiss on the cheek. I think that you are never too cool to give your mom or dad a kiss.

I also think this generation has forgotten about dinnertime. I love dinner. My wife cooks. I love to sit at the table with the kids. Unfortunately, it seems like dinnertime is disappearing. Everyone is in a rush. Everyone is looking at their phones. Everyone has got their iPads. That stuff is put away when we have dinner. We talk about our favorite part of our day. We enjoy being together. You develop a bond. If there is one piece of advice that I would give to families, try and have dinner together and talk about your day. Kids love that.

The Takeaway: Put the Devices Down for Dinner

We are all caught up in a world of instant gratification. We feel that since we have the technology to stay connected to our work that we need to respond right away to that "important" email or text. You don't.

The next time you and your family are eating dinner together, look around the table. What is everyone doing? If they're staring at a phone, tablet, or TV screen, have everyone turn them off and do something crazy…just talk to each other. Make that time a priority where you're solely focused on your kids and you'll be surprised—they will do the same for you.

When It Comes to Your Kids Playing Sports, Relax
Rick Reilly

DADOGRAPHY

Twitter: @ReillyRick
Born: February 3, 1958
Kids: 3
Career: *New York Times* Bestselling Author, Legendary Sportswriter

For a generation of sports fans, Rick Reilly occupied arguably the most valuable real estate in sports: the back-page column in *Sports Illustrated*. Talk to die-hard *SI* readers from the 1990s, and half of them will jokingly tell you they either learned to read from Reilly's columns or only read Reilly's columns. And he wasn't just a fan favorite. The media industry as a whole recognized Reilly's skills, naming him National Sportswriter of the Year an incredible eleven times.

He has published a dozen books, many of which were *New York Times* bestsellers, in addition to writing screenplays and hosting shows on ESPN. He also used his influence to found Nothing But Nets, an organization that has raised millions of dollars to hang mosquito nets in Africa to protect kids from getting malaria.

While the professional focus of Reilly's career has been to write about other people's lives, accomplishments, families, and foibles, he is the father of three, has a wicked self-deprecating humor, and says that after forty years writing a weekly sports column and raising three kids, if he could give dads advice, it would be to take everything a little easier.

LOD: You've been writing about professional sports for forty years. What advice do you have for dads who are navigating the youth athletic landscape?

RR: Well, I did a column called "Truth." It is about things that I know to be true after thirty-seven years of doing this. One is that your kid is not going to remember a single score of any game he ever played. He is going to remember the time that Capri Sun came out of his nose in the dugout. So, just relax. It is not going to matter. You are not going to win every game. Let him have fun. He is not going pro. If you ever use the word "us" in regards to your kid's team, you are too into it. Back off.

I always say this about raising kids. Everyone is trying to get to Heaven. I told my kids once that everyone is trying to get to Heaven, but I think that Heaven is the actual journey.

Maybe paradise is just catching pop-ups or your kid sister in a bicycle helmet two sizes too big or tackle basketball with your family. All that stuff is what stayed with them. All my kids are grown up. We still talk about the Nerf wars we had or the games of hide and seek. It was never about "Did we win the championship?" or "Did you get a 1600 on your SAT?" I wish parents would relax more and just enjoy the journey.

The Takeaway: When Kids Are Little, Prioritize Fun, Not Winning

Any dads reading this who have coached one of their young kids' teams can testify that he is 100-percent dead-on about this. Yes, learning how to compete and learning how to lose and how to win are valuable life skills, and sports are a fantastic way to teach them. But most likely your kid is not going pro. He or she won't remember the tie game or the big win or the huge loss. They'll remember the kid who got stung by a bee or the time a coach fell leaving the dugout. Or the basketball game you invented together in the driveway. These things are just facts. So, relax about the score. The score is just the end result. The joy, as Reilly says, is in the journey.

Quality Time and Quantity Time Matter
David Robinson

DADOGRAPHY

Twitter: @DavidtheAdmiral
Born: August 6, 1965
Kids: Corey, David Jr., Justin
Career: NBA Hall of Famer, Entrepreneur

David Robinson is one of the most unique, inspiring athletes the American sports landscape has ever produced. He was drafted by the San Antonio Spurs with the first overall pick in the 1987 NBA Draft (after having only started playing basketball as a senior in high school), but the league would have to wait while he fulfilled his active-duty obligation to the US Naval Academy, where he graduated from.

Following his time as a civil engineering officer, he joined the Spurs, promptly won Rookie of the Year, and then went on one of the most successful runs the sport has ever seen over the course of the next fifteen years. He won two Olympic gold medals, two NBA championships, an MVP award, a scoring title, ten All-NBA team nominations and ten All-Star selections, culminating in his being voted into the Pro Basketball Hall of Fame and having his number retired by San Antonio.

More importantly, along the way he picked up several Sportsperson of the Year awards from various outlets, including *Sports Illustrated*, and became the father of three boys. Often held up as one of the most thoughtful, intelligent, and strongest role models in the NBA, Robinson offered some interesting thoughts on what it means to be a dad and spend time with your kids.

LOD: You had a long and successful NBA career that required a lot of travel while your sons were young—however, you have a great relationship with your boys. How were you able to build that and what advice would you give other dads in a similar situation?

DR: The number one thing that I would say is, don't buy that little argument about quality time and quantity time. Quantity time is quality time. Being there is way more important than you think. I understand if you are in the military. You've got to be away. My father had to be away. Kids are resilient. They will bounce back and figure things out.

But if you can be there, then be there. That is just the bottom line. If you have the choice to spend time with your children, spend time with your children. I guarantee you that you will never, ever regret it. That would be the number one thing that I would say for young dads. If you can't be there, don't feel guilty about it. That is something that you can't control. Like I said, kids are very resilient. They will be fine, but they will also know that you couldn't be there. If you can be there but aren't, they will know that you could be there but decided not to be there.

The Takeaway: Admiring the Admiral's Take on Time

Sometimes we don't question the old sayings we've heard a thousand times because we just assume that the reason they're repeated so often is because they're true. The use of the phrase "quality time" to describe time spent with our family and our kids has been drilled into our heads so long we could be forgiven for just accepting that it matters more than anything else. But to Robinson's point, so does simply being there. And so does showing your children that when you have a choice, you choose them. Making that choice over and over again will result in both: quantity time and quality time. Think about it.

Learning from Athletes and Their Dads
Gary Myers

DADOGRAPHY

Twitter: @GaryMyersNY
Born: August 15, 1952
Kids: 3
Career: Author, Sports Journalist

Gary Myers was practically an institution unto himself inside the sports pages of the *New York Daily News*. He spent twenty-nine years as a sportswriter at the paper, covering the NFL and the New York Giants. He's also appeared on HBO's *Inside the NFL* as well as the YES Network.

As an author, Myers is a *New York Times* bestseller, having penned *The Catch*, about the 1981 NFC Championship Game between the Dallas Cowboys and the San Francisco 49ers, *Coaching Confidential*, and *Brady vs. Manning*, about the greatest quarterback rivalry in the history of the league.

Myers's book *My First Coach: Inspiring Stories of NFL Quarterbacks and Their Dads* is right in our wheelhouse as he examines the father-son relationships of the Mannings, the Elways, the Harbaughs, the Simms, the Montanas, and more. While researching the book and interviewing the high-achieving sons and the fathers behind them, he got a first-hand look at some of the strategies these dads employed while raising prodigies.

LOD: Did you discover any commonalities or themes among the fathers who raised NFL quarterbacks in your book?

GM: For the most part, these fathers were very supportive of their sons' athletic endeavors—whether they coached them or were there for moral support. They all were able to lean on their fathers to help them with any issues that they had.

Jameis Winston's dad was tough on him. He felt that he would never do anything that would satisfy him on the field because his dad was always pushing him to be the best that he could be. Derek Carr's father, on the other hand, even when Derek would play a bad game in high school, all he would do is point out the good things that he did. I think that they responded to the type of father that they had. I think that Jameis is an extremely hard worker. Derek is now one of the highest paid players in NFL history.

I was able to relate to a lot of the stories in the book. My son just graduated college. He was a very good baseball player, but he wasn't going to take it any further than that. At the age of ten or eleven, I didn't know that. I encouraged him the same way that Joe Montana's dad encouraged him and the same way Tom Brady's dad encouraged him.

The Takeaway: Whether You're "Coach" or "Dad," Be There

No parent of a gifted athlete truly knows if their ten-year-old son or daughter is a prodigy or just really good for their age. There's no way to tell if high school will be the peak of their athletic career or if college will or if they'll completely topple the odds and play a sport professionally. As Myers found out in his book, whether it was Joe Montana's dad or Tom Brady's dad or Jameis Winston's dad, your job is to be there as the one person your child can count on and talk to about anything as their career goes in whatever direction it's meant to go.

Find Time to Laugh with Your Wife
Channing Frye

DADOGRAPHY

Twitter: @Channing_Frye
Born: May 17, 1983
Kids: Margaux, Hendrix
Career: NBA Player, Philanthropist

After playing for five teams in roughly ten NBA seasons, Channing Frye won a championship with LeBron James and the Cleveland Cavaliers in 2016. By that point, he had spent significant time with the Orlando Magic, Phoenix Suns, Portland Trail Blazers, and New York Knicks, who selected him eighth overall in the 2005 NBA Draft.

In 2010, along with his wife Lauren, Frye created the Frye Family Foundation to give back to local communities. This was the second charity he founded. The first was the Channing Frye Foundation, which was dedicated to improving the lives and positivity of kids. Frye is also the father of two kids, who he has worked hard to maintain a regular relationship and presence with despite his heavy road schedule. He also has an interesting game plan to keep things light and upbeat.

LOD: The NBA lifestyle involves a lot of travel and time away from your family. What are your strategies with your wife and kids to maintain a strong relationship?

CF: My wife is an absolute saint. She knows that this life is very short-lived and does the best job I have ever seen. She makes sure the kids watch all my games, and she watches them with our friends and family. My interaction with them is extremely important. She also knows that this is business and I get pretty serious on game day. We Skype on days that I have off when I have long road trips, but on game days it is like zero contact with the outside world.

I want my kids and my family to just have fun. Life is short, and it could be taken away in the blink of an eye. My wife and I have found that when you laugh and are having fun, it makes things so much more memorable. Life is hard at times, and if you can laugh even for five minutes, it's great. Watch a funny video together, like someone farting or something. It will cheer you up. Everyone loves a good fart joke.

The Takeaway: The Fart Joke Unites Us All

A prerequisite for being in the *Life of Dad* community is the ability to laugh at a good fart joke (are there any bad ones?). On that note, we naturally think Frye has a good point. So many tips and tactics involving keeping a strong relationship with your kids or your spouse can quickly become serious and involve words like *priorities* and *attention*, and that's valid. Sometimes, though…staying connected with your significant other, even if you're on the road, can come down to sharing a great fart video and laughing about it together.

Remember to Protect Your Adult Time and Relationship
Jonathan Auxier

DADOGRAPHY

Twitter: @JonathanAuxier
Born: 1980
Kids: 3 daughters
Career: Author

If you or your children have ever joined Peter Nimble (and his fantastic eyes) on a rollicking journey, then you're already a fan of *New York Times* bestselling author Jonathan Auxier and one of his central characters. If you aren't familiar, then we'd highly recommend you start with his first book, *The Night Gardener*, which won a Canadian Library Association Book of the Year for Children award in 2014. After that, you can dive headfirst into the Peter Nimble series and we promise you (and your kids) won't regret it.

Auxier, a Canadian who now lives in Pittsburgh, told us he got his creativity from his own father, who he says, "is a natural storyteller. He is an unflappable, fun person. He reminds me in a less extreme way of the dad in the Roald Dahl book, *Danny, the Champion of the World.*"

Auxier is the father of three daughters, and his goal is to model himself after his own dad and to model his marriage after his parents' marriage, since they had a very strong bond. One of his main strategies to do that is to make sure he and his wife pay as much attention to their relationship as they do to their kids.

LOD: You've spoken very highly of your dad and the great relationship he had with your mom. What are some of the things you do to model your family along that path?

JA: One of the things that my wife and I were very aggressive about was maintaining our relationship above every other thing. We are making sure that it is never something that we ignore or neglect.

That is something that my parents modeled. It is not always easy to do. I do believe that a strong spousal relationship is probably the greatest gift you can give your child. I say that as a recipient of that in my own life. So, in many ways, the best thing for a new parent is to forget about the child once in a while and focus on their marriage relationship. I think the child will feel that security. That is not always doable, and I understand that.

When you are a new parent, I think you can get so focused on this little creature that you have to keep alive that it becomes your only common ground. I plan to have much more life than the years my child is living under my roof, just as I had a whole lot of life before my child appeared in my life.

The Takeaway: It's Okay to Look Out for You and Your Spouse

The calls to "put kids first no matter what" are often the loudest and come without any real pushback from those who believe that kids benefit a great deal from a household where the parents have a strong, loving relationship. The mom and dad who are running all over town to get their kids to activities and who spend the weekends apart at different games/tournaments/events while spending the week apart while at work is almost cliché at this point, but sadly, it's true.

Keep in mind that there are no points awarded for "most dedicated parent," especially if it comes at the expense of your relationship with your partner. While we all want to support our kids, make sure you carve out not only time but space for you and your partner to be together without the kids around. In the long run, they'll thank you for it.

Staying on the Same Page As Mom
Jeff "Swampy" Marsh

DADOGRAPHY

Twitter: @MMonogram
Born: December 9, 1960
Kids: 1 daughter, 1 son
Career: Animator, Writer, Producer, Director, Voice Actor

In terms of having a strong pedigree in animation, it doesn't get any bigger than *The Simpsons* and *King of the Hill*. Animator/director/voice actor/producer Jeff "Swampy" Marsh worked on both. And while that will surely impress you, what will impress your kids is that Marsh was an executive producer for the Disney Channel's *Phineas and Ferb* and is also the voice behind the Major Francis Monogram character.

Most recently, Marsh was the show runner for Amazon Prime Video's *Pete the Cat: A Groovy New Year*, based on the hit book series. The father of two lives in Venice, California, is an avid surfer, and one of his great joys is being able to work with his son, who does voice work on some of his projects. "It is the best," he told us about collaborating with his son. "I have to say that I am immensely proud of my son. He is one of the easiest guys to work with. It is one of the reasons why we keep on working together. It is a joy. He works hard. He stays focused. We always laugh together and yet we push really hard."

Marsh's two children are far apart in age, and one piece of advice he shares with us involves maintaining a united front as parents.

LOD: You've built a strong-enough relationship with your son, and he clearly has an admirable work ethic and respect for you. What is one thing you've done to raise such a well-rounded kid?

JM: Make sure that you and mom are on the same page. Have those conversations. It doesn't necessarily mean that you have to agree. You guys have to find a solution [to any issue] before, so by the time you come to your child you have a consensus and you are consistent. One thing that I have said to my son quite recently when there was an issue going on was, "Look, the one thing that I can always do is be honest with you. It doesn't mean you are always going to like what I say, but I am always going to be honest with you. You can count on that."

I think a lot of that comes with you and mom being on the same page and really taking the time to talk it through. Make sure that all the decisions that you make are not the ones that will just benefit you in the next five minutes, next hour, or next day. My wife and I try to make sure we think about how the decision we make today will potentially affect him in five years or ten years. That comes with sitting down and talking to him.

We spent late nights sitting up and talking and thinking about what are we going to do about this, that, and the other thing. That seems to be what has paid off more than anything else. My son knows that we have a consistent message to him and he can count on that.

The Takeaway: Agree to Disagree Away from Your Kids

Marsh's advice to take the time to work out any disagreement regarding an issue with your kids before you actually talk to them is some of the best we've heard. When it comes to major decisions or choices you have to make that affect your kids, be it a punishment or consent to do something, they can tell if you and your spouse don't agree and they'll side with one of you or paint one of you as "the bad guy."

Like Marsh said, you and your spouse will not agree on every course of action, and that's totally normal. The key is to work that out ahead of time, so that you agree in front of your kids, and they'll know they can't play you off of each other. This strategy will foster equal respect for both of you.

CHAPTER 9

Handling Challenges

"When adversity strikes, that's when you have to be most calm. Take a step back, stay strong, stay grounded, and press on."
—LL Cool J, Father of Four

Having Faith and Finding Blessings
Jim Kelly

DADOGRAPHY

Twitter: @JimKelly1212
Born: February 14, 1960
Kids: Hunter, Erin, Camryn
Career: Philanthropist, NFL Hall of Famer

Because of the nature of this topic, we're going to handle the sharing of our interview with Jim Kelly a little differently and essentially give him the floor here. Kelly is a Pro Football Hall of Fame quarterback who took his team to four straight Super Bowls (a feat no other team has done), although the Buffalo Bills didn't win any of them. He made five Pro Bowls (in addition to two USFL All-League teams) and led the NFL in passing touchdowns in 1991. He is also a three-time cancer survivor, and in this interview, while we did talk a lot of football, we also discussed his son, Hunter, who was born with (and ultimately passed away from) Krabbe disease.

LOD: This is a very sensitive topic and we appreciate you sharing. For fathers out there who have children with special needs or who are battling illness, we'd like to give you the chance to share what you went through and how you coped.

JK: Mothers and fathers look at different things different ways. My wife Jill and I handled it totally different. She handled it like a mother would. I handled it like what I thought a father would. Turns out, I needed to get a little closer to the situation and humble myself to know that I had to be able to communicate.

I don't know what the divorce rate is for families with a special needs child, but I know it is not great. You just have to be able to talk things out, and if you need counseling, go to counseling. My wife and I needed it. I didn't think I needed that. I thought, "I know what I am doing. I played football." Bull. You need to be able to talk things out. Counseling can really help. I had to humble myself to understand that there were things that I was doing wrong. Communication between mom and dad, husband and wife is so crucial for keeping a happy family. Until you talk it out, you will never get to where you need to be.

Eventually, I understood that this was God's will and I also had to stay strong for my spouse. Too many men forget to check their ego. They let the macho part take over instead of really understanding what the wife and the mother goes through and understand what they can do to help.

My son is now in Heaven. He passed away at the age of eight. Even though my son never spoke a word, never moved a muscle in his body, he didn't have to. He made me a lot better person than I was, a lot better man today than I was many years ago. He taught me so much.

I thank the good Lord every day for my son, even though he was almost like a sacrifice through him and through me to make a difference in other kids. When you see that in every appearance that you make and you see families walking up to you and holding their children in their arms and thanking you, then you understand why the good Lord picked me as a special father of a little special boy named Hunter so we can make a difference for other families.

The Takeaway: Be Open to Being Humbled

We are in awe of how open and honest Kelly was with us about the issues he dealt with regarding his son, Hunter. We are grateful he shared with us, and if you are going through something similar with your child we hope his words helped in some way. His thoughts really make you grateful for what you have in life, and help you stay open to seeing blessings where you might not expect them.

Staying On Top of Your Health and Tackling Problems Head-On

Aaron Boone

DADOGRAPHY

Twitter: @AaronBoone
Born: March 9, 1973
Kids: 2
Career: MLB Manager, MLB Player

Before taking over one of the most prestigious jobs in all of sports (as the manager of the New York Yankees) and before retiring as a Major League Baseball player (after a career that spanned six teams and delivering one of the most soul-sucking, city-crushing, game-winning home runs ever to beat the Boston Red Sox in the 2003 American League Championship Series), Aaron Boone was just a kid in college taking up the family business: baseball.

Boone is the brother of Bret Boone, a four-time MLB All-Star; the son of Bob Boone, a longtime MLB player; and the grandson of Ray Boone, an infielder who spent twelve years in the majors. While in college at the University of Southern California, he discovered that he had a congenital heart defect and that one day he would likely need surgery. Boone is the father of four children and shared with us what living with a heart condition was like, as well as thoughts on his surgery and recovery.

LOD: You had been monitoring your heart condition for two decades before you had to address it with surgery. Can you tell us your thoughts on what the process was like and how you handled the procedure? What helped the most?

AB: The fact that I knew about my situation for twenty years was helpful. I did my due diligence of getting my checkups, so doctors were on top of the growth of my heart and knew when I actually needed to have the surgeries. Maybe twenty to forty years before that, they wouldn't have been able to detect it, and it would have turned into a heart attack or a stroke. With all the advancements and the great technology available, you can prevent catastrophic situations by being aware, by getting checked out, and by monitoring not only what is going on with your heart but with the rest of your body.

With the surgery, I knew that day was out there someday. When they tell you that the time has come, it still hits you pretty hard. The reality of something major that you've got to tackle and take on. It happened right in spring training when I was getting ready for the season, so I didn't expect it.

It definitely is a wake-up call. At the same time, I was very eager to get it done. I had different injuries throughout my career, obviously not related to the heart. I knew that this was a big one. I had a ton of confidence in my doctor, my surgeons, and all the people up in Stamford who did my procedure. I was very much at peace going in knowing I was in good hands and ultimately God's hands.

I was at peace if this was the end of my career. I was going to be fine with that. That being said, once I had the surgery and the recovery and rehab process was going well, they green-lit me to try and get back.

It was very gratifying to see your body go through open heart surgery and all that it entails; to undergo weight loss but see your body return over a few months; to work hard at the gym to get back and play in the month of September. It was my going-out party, if you will. It was my only year in Houston, but I ended up playing with a lot of people that I am still close with who were so supportive.

It is in times like that where you really appreciate friendships and people who are trying to enable you, help you, and support you in realizing your dream in getting back. The fact that I was able to do that was a little bit of closure for me in my career.

With medicine and technology now, you can find out what is going on with your body at early stages of things. Early detection can really help you fulfill your goals and get the most out of your life.

The Takeaway: Stay On Top of Your Health and Trust the Plan

Too many dads try to "tough out" health issues that they're dealing with by delaying going to the doctor or not going at all. We put our jobs, our families, and even our hobbies over our own health sometimes and that can be a catastrophic mistake. Simply put, if something doesn't feel right, get it checked out and monitor it. Then follow the plan you and your doctor lay out for treatment.

Reach Out for Help and Make a Difference
Boomer Esiason

DADOGRAPHY

Twitter: @7BoomerEsiason
Born: April 17, 1961
Kids: 2
Career: NFL Quarterback, TV Analyst, Radio Host, Philanthropist

Boomer Esiason played quarterback in the NFL for fourteen years, including nine years with a classic Cincinnati Bengals team that was among the highest scoring squads in the NFL. The four-time Pro Bowler and 1988 league MVP also played briefly for the New York Jets and the Arizona Cardinals. After retirement, Esiason joined the popular CBS pregame football show and also hosts the *Boomer and Gio* morning radio show in New York City.

However, despite all of this, if you ask Esiason what accomplishment he is the proudest of, he would say it's the work he does through his organization, which looks to support and improve the lives of those who have cystic fibrosis. His son, Gunnar, was diagnosed with cystic fibrosis (CF) in 1993, and Esiason has used his popularity and platform to raise awareness for the disease to help his son and other children who have CF.

LOD: Your work with children who have cystic fibrosis is inspiring to dads everywhere. Did your involvement start with your son's diagnosis? We appreciate you sharing what the experience has been like for you.

BE: I was actually exposed to cystic fibrosis in 1989 by Frank Deford [a sports-writer and author]. Frank was speaking at a banquet that I was at. He had lost his daughter Alex to cystic fibrosis. Cystic fibrosis is a genetically transmitted disease. My wife and I didn't know that we carried the recessive gene trait.

The disease itself involves the lungs and the digestive system. The lungs are marked with bacterial infection. When Gunnar was diagnosed in 1993 at the age of two, when I became the quarterback of the Jets, the second phone call I made was to Frank Deford. He was just as shocked as I was that destiny and irony had found our family when Gunnar was diagnosed with the disease that ultimately killed his daughter.

He said that this was God's way of saying that we have an opportunity here to use your celebrity in New York to raise funds and awareness for cystic fibrosis. I have always taken that piece of advice as seriously as it deserved to be taken. After twenty years of watching Gunnar grow up and graduate from Boston College, I feel really strongly that we have taken Frank's ideas and have tried to create a world in which cystic fibrosis patients can live a healthy, normal, and productive life, just like any child in the world.

Watching Gunnar fight this disease every day, I am most proud as a dad of what he has already accomplished in his young life. I want him to become a father himself. As any father can attest to, there is nothing more fulfilling.

We are trying to make a difference in the lives of cystic fibrosis patients. Gunnar is a prime example of that. I think we have accomplished our mission, but the ultimate goal is to cure this disease, and we are still a ways from that.

In the past twenty years, the average lifespan of a person with cystic fibrosis went from nineteen to thirty-seven. Even though it is not easy living with cystic fibrosis, as Gunnar has proven and many young adults like him have proven, it is an attitude that you have to have. You've got to be positive. You've got to be realistic. You've got to be aggressive in dealing with the disease. That is one of the reasons that we are seeing kids live a lot longer. We are seeing female CF patients being able to deliver their own babies and becoming moms themselves. It is really becoming quite the story. We have a number of CF patients who run in marathons. The story of triumph in the world of cystic fibrosis has really been nothing short of a miracle thus far.

The Takeaway: Get Help, Get Educated, and Get to Work Making a Difference

When it comes to raising a child with a disease like cystic fibrosis, parents all have their own coping mechanisms and far be it for us to tell anyone what to do. All we can say is that Esiason's strategy to immediately reach out to another father he knew who dealt with the same thing, and then to pour himself into understanding the disease so he could do everything he could to improve his son's life, worked for him. If you're reading this and going through a similar situation, maybe it will work for you too.

Dealing with Illness:
Focus On Your Position and Not Your Condition
Chuck Pagano

DADOGRAPHY
Born: October 2, 1960
Kids: 3
Career: NFL Head Coach

From the start of Chuck Pagano's coaching career as a graduate assistant for the University of Southern California in 1984 to the time he was named an NFL head coach for the Indianapolis Colts in 2012, he held thirteen different coaching jobs in nine states. During that twenty-eight-year span, Pagano embraced every opportunity that came his way, jumping from Los Angeles to Miami to Boise to Las Vegas and on and on until he reached his goal of becoming an NFL head coach.

Persistence and perseverance, as you can see, were not issues with Pagano. When he finally got the call from the Colts, it seemed a lifetime of hard work was paying off. Yes, he was inheriting a team who just lost an all-time NFL legend in Peyton Manning, but no matter. He had one of the thirty-two most coveted coaching jobs in football.

In the third week of the first season of his first job as NFL head coach, he found out he had cancer. Specifically, acute promyelocytic leukemia (APL). He was floored. He ended up missing the next eight weeks to undergo chemotherapy, and, fortunately, he regained his health and was able to finish the season and resume his coaching career. But that's the happy ending. The journey wasn't easy. While he details his story in his book, *Sidelined*, he talked to us about the mindset that he found necessary to get through this difficult time.

LOD: There's a quote in your book that reads, "Recognizing with gratitude the many blessings in life is critical to keeping a positive attitude." Can you reflect on what that meant to you as you battled cancer and what it can mean for others going through the same thing?

CP: There is never a specific time that I don't think about those words. I have never really taken anything for granted, ever. Going through what we went through as an organization, as a team, and as a family...I think it just puts things in perspective. We are not guaranteed tomorrow. We all know that. So we are going to take care of every day, every minute we have on this Earth.

When you first get diagnosed, you have a couple of minutes there with the doctor. He is telling you that you have the APL form of leukemia.

He tells you what you have to go through in order to get treatment and beat this.

Then you come back to your wife and kids. I have a beautiful wife, three kids, and three granddaughters. My sole motivation and inspiration was that I signed up for that, for life. They are counting on me to be there. Certainly, I have got to finish the job. My team—from the owner to the coaches, like Bruce (Arians), the players, the city, this community, and the fans—they didn't know me yet. I hadn't been there long when I got diagnosed. The way they embraced me and my family is a debt that I will never be able to repay.

I live in vision and not circumstance. We are all going to be faced with adversity, whether it is being diagnosed with some disease or dealing with a tragedy in your family. Life is tough. You have to focus on your position and not your condition. My condition was that I was diagnosed with leukemia. My position was that I was going to beat this and be around for a long time for my family and my loved ones. If anyone can take anything from my book, it is to live in vision and not circumstance. Focus on your position. It is all about your attitude and your will to win and overcome.

The Takeaway: Live in Vision, Not Circumstance

There are several powerful ideas that Pagano covers while discussing his fight with cancer, but that phrase, "live in vision, not circumstance," truly hit us hard. No matter what you're going through or a family member is going through, understand where you are in the moment and focus on the positive mindset of where you want to be. Pagano focused on his family and finishing the job he arrived in Indianapolis to do. That worked for him. You need to find what will work for you.

THE LIFE OF DAD

How to Overcome Abuse and Thrive
Steve Costello

DADOGRAPHY

Born: 1966
Kids: 2
Career: Author, Sports Marketing Executive, Motivational Speaker

As a longtime executive for Steiner Sports Marketing, Steve Costello regularly rubbed elbows with some of the biggest-name athletes, from Yankees legends like Derek Jeter and Mariano Rivera to Eli Manning and even iconic basketball coach Bob Knight. For a kid who grew up worshipping at the altar of sports, particularly baseball, the career was a dream come true. But in addition to loving America's pastime for the home runs and strikeouts and diving catches, Costello also used the game as a means of escape from a childhood of abuse.

As described in his book, *My Father Never Took Me to a Baseball Game,* Costello was the victim of mental child abuse at home and bullying at school. Now the father of two grown-up girls, he talked to us about what his childhood situation was like, how he coped, and how it affected his own thoughts on being a dad.

LOD: You've gone into great detail in your book about how you handled the abuse from your father and bullies as a child. What thoughts do you have for someone reading this who went through a similar situation?

SC: Growing up in the '60s, it was a much different environment. My mom didn't drive. My mom didn't have a job. She had three sons—where do you even go? My mom didn't have an outlet. We didn't have an outlet.

I would go from the stuff with my dad to the stuff with my friends, which I outline in the book. It was different levels of bullying. There is a part in the book where my friends treated me so badly, but then I was the only one of my friends to make the basketball team. It kind of shut them up. It taught me the lesson that actions are more powerful than words.

What I am finding out from people who are reading my book is that if you were physically or mentally abused as a kid, you don't have to be ashamed of it because you had nothing to do with it. You really didn't have a choice. I took all of the lessons from that, and when I had my own children, I decided that I was going to break the chain.

I was going to be a pacifist, very educated, and a very chill dad. I pulled it off. That is why after reading my book, my daughter insisted on making an afterword. It just blew me away. She wrote about her feelings. I found out later that my younger daughter even took the ferry up to Boston to help her with it. That is just more than you can imagine as a dad.

The Takeaway: Break the Chain

One of the most heartbreaking aspects of abuse is when an abused child grows up to be an abusive parent. Costello has done a lot of personal work to recognize that he shouldn't feel ashamed about being abused because it wasn't his fault. He didn't choose his father… but he could choose what kind of father he wanted to be. He chose to break the chain.

Being Strong for Your Family
Charles "Peanut" Tillman

DADOGRAPHY

Twitter: @PeanutTillman
Born: February 23, 1981
Kids: 2
Career: NFL Player, Media Host, FBI Agent

Charles Tillman and "Peanut" Tillman are alter egos of the same person. "Peanut" Tillman is the football player who spent a majority of his career with the Chicago Bears and won his share of on-field awards, including two Pro Bowl selections and a first-team All-Pro selection. But Charles Tillman, the leader and philanthropist, has earned even more recognition, winning the prestigious Walter Payton NFL Man of the Year Award in 2013 for his stellar volunteer and charity work. Charles is also a three-time Brian Piccolo Award winner, which exemplifies the courage, loyalty, teamwork, dedication, and sense of humor of the late Brian Piccolo, a former Bears running back.

The Charles Tillman Cornerstone Foundation, founded in 2005 to help provide opportunities and resources to families with chronically ill or critically ill children, has helped thousands of families. When Tillman discovered his daughter, Tiana, was born with a congenital heart defect (CHD), he began work with the Saving tiny Hearts Society as well. He spoke to us about how Tiana's journey has changed his life.

LOD: What were your first thoughts when you found out your daughter had CHD, and what advice can you give other dads going through something similar with their own children?

CT: *First initial thought? It was, "Holy damn." There is so much emotion running through you. You are in shock. You are in awe. You are like, "Wow, is this really happening to me? Is she going to die? Does she need a heart transplant? Is she sick?" I had a million thoughts. I was trying to process them all at one time. I remember the doctor telling me the news. I went to the bathroom. I literally just broke down. I absolutely lost it. I broke down as if she had already died.*

Then I took a deep breath and splashed some water on my face. I slapped myself in the face. I looked in the mirror and said, "Come on." I was actually having a conversation with myself. It was a conversation between Charles and Peanut. We were having a dialogue. I told myself to get it together. You have to take care of your family. Man up. Let's go. From that point on I tried to be the man I could be and protect my family. I was trying to give them that security of knowing that everything was going to be okay.

The best advice that I can give is, "Accept it." What you are going through is your new normal. Once you accept that fact that your kid has a congenital heart defect and that they will need surgery, you will be thinking, "How am I going to deal with the demands, the crazy schedule, and the tubes?" I remember waking up every three hours to give my daughter her meds when she got out of the hospital. But you adjust. It will become your new normal like anything else.

You can still live a normal life. Your child will be able to do things. Maybe not everything that the other kids are doing, but for the most part your child can live a normal life. You get to be happy and take trips. Everything will be good.

The first year or two were really tough, but you just get used to it. It wears on you from time to time, but in the end, if she is alive, you think, "I don't care what it takes. If I have to wake up in the middle of the night to give her some meds, that is the least of my worries." You start to see the bigger picture. My daughter's heart defect made me grow up more and see life in a different way.

The Takeaway: Accept the New Normal

Whether you need to have a dialogue with yourself or you need time on your own to adjust to your "new normal," we're grateful for Tillman's honesty in talking about such a tough subject. His decision to face the challenge head-on and embrace her care helped him accept her condition and be grateful for her life. We hope his vulnerability regarding his initial thoughts and how he has coped will provide some measure of help if you find yourself in a similar situation.

Handling Challenges Together
Dick Hoyt

DADOGRAPHY

Born: June 1, 1940
Kids: 2
Career: Ultra Athlete, Philanthropist

Dick Hoyt has competed in more than 1,200 endurance events with his son Rick, including over seventy marathons and seven Ironman Triathlons. They have raced in the Boston Marathon thirty-two times. They once biked and ran across the United States, completing 3,735 miles in forty-five days.

Pretty impressive, right? Wait until you hear the catch. Rick Hoyt was born with cerebral palsy, and Dick either pushes or pulls him throughout each race and challenge.

The Hoyts have been competing together for more than forty years, and it all began with a simple request. Back in 1977, after Rick heard about a local lacrosse player being paralyzed, he asked his father if they could compete in a five-mile benefit run for the player.

Dick agreed and pushed his son in his wheelchair across the finish line for their first race. When it was over, Rick told his dad, "When I'm running, it feels like I'm not handicapped."

That was all Dick needed to hear. He began running every day with a bag of cement in a wheelchair to train while Rick was in school. The two have won numerous awards over the years and have become celebrities in the endurance and ultra-athlete world. None of this would have happened if Dick had listened to his son's doctor's original advice.

LOD: Your story is one of true love and dedication between a father and a son. What was the beginning of your journey like, and what have you learned along the way?

DH: When Rick was born in 1962, the umbilical cord got twisted around his neck. That caused a lack of oxygen to Rick's brain, which caused brain damage, which is cerebral palsy. At the time we knew something was wrong with Rick, but we didn't know exactly what.

So the doctor made an appointment with us to see a specialist when Rick was eight months old. We took Rick to the specialist and they did all kinds of tests. The test came back very negative. The doctors told us to put Rick in an institution because he is going to be nothing but a vegetable for the rest of his life. Today, Rick is in his fifties. We still haven't figured out what vegetable he is.

On our way home from that doctor's appointment, my wife and I cried. We talked. We said, "No—we are not going to put Rick away. We are going to bring him home and raise him up like any other child." Rick has been mainstreamed and included all of his life.

He has graduated from public high school. He has graduated from Boston University. He lives all by himself in his own apartment. Rick and I have competed in over 1,200 athletic events in the past twenty-two years. The biggest thing that we wanted to do was get Rick an education. We wanted him to go to the regular schools with all the other children.

My inspiration has been Rick. Rick is a fighter. He is not a quitter. He is never going to quit. Our message to him is, "Yes, you can. There isn't anything that you can't do as long as you make up your mind to do it."

The Takeaway: You Can Do Anything

All you have to do is Google "Team Hoyt" to get a visual of the Hoyts in competition and understand what they have overcome together. The lesson, as the Hoyts said, is to never let anyone put limitations on what you or your kids can accomplish. We love the idea of entering races and competitions together as a way to build your relationship with your kids, regardless of hardship. And if you need any inspiration, read their book: *Devoted: The Story of a Father's Love for His Son.*

Accepting and Understanding Your Child's Illness
Mark Feuerstein

DADOGRAPHY

Twitter: @markfeuerstein
Born: June 8, 1971
Kids: 3
Career: Actor

Lawyer. Doctor. Rogue CIA agent. Actor Mark Feuerstein defines "range" when it comes to his roles on hit TV shows like *The West Wing, Royal Pains,* and *Prison Break*. He also starred in one season of a sitcom based on his own real-life experience while filming *Royal Pains*, called *9JKL*.

When he's not on camera, Feuerstein is often outside, either hiking with one of his kids, coaching, mountain biking, or competing in one of the six Malibu Triathlons he has competed in to raise money for Children's Hospital Los Angeles (CHLA). That particular hospital holds personal significance for Feuerstein, as the doctors there saved his daughter's life after she was diagnosed with a heart condition. In our interview, the actor tells us what it was like the day he found out about his daughter's serious health problem.

LOD: You've been very candid sharing the experience you and your wife went through with your daughter, Addy, and her heart problems. Thankfully, she's doing well now, but if you can take us back to the beginning for fathers reading this dealing with the same thing, we'd appreciate it.

MF: Man, the hardest thing that can ever happen to a mother or father is to watch their child suffering. I was in the middle of shooting season two of Royal Pains. *I had to leave the hospital to go to Puerto Rico to shoot. I just witnessed my child having open-heart surgery, the first of her two.*

When we found out, it was just a random day in L.A. I was doing some DVD commentary on some ridiculous movie that I did for the WWE with the Big Show. *When I got out onto Burbank Boulevard, my wife calls me. We had been trying to figure out why Addy wasn't gaining weight. They thought it was reflux. I said, "It is okay, honey, relax. It is just the reflux. We have been to an endocrinologist. We have been to a gastroenterologist." But my wife was very rigorous. She said, "The reflux medicine isn't helping. She isn't gaining weight."*

She had an appointment with a cardiologist that afternoon. As hard as this is to admit, she asked me if she should go. I told her that she didn't have to go. I said, "If you want to and it works in your day, go." She said that she would go. That afternoon after the DVD commentary, I get a call from my wife screaming that we have to go to Children's

Hospital immediately because Addy needs open heart surgery. She has a rare congenital heart defect called ALCAPA, which stands for anomalous left coronary artery from the pulmonary artery. There is one guy who can do it: Dr. Vaughn Starnes. He is the same doctor that operated on Jimmy Kimmel's son and saved his life. He saves about five to seven children's hearts a day. When I am quibbling over a joke in a scene, I just remember that. The joke doesn't really matter.

He operated once. Addy was in the cardiothoracic intensive care unit for eighty-nine days, taking one step forward and then two steps back. It was the worst summer of our lives. I was flying home every single weekend and every single day off from New York....She was not doing well until he performed her second surgery. That one did the trick.

A week after the second surgery, she was looking so much better. She started getting off of all of those horrible pumps that they have in a hospital room. She was home a month later. She was eating. Now she is the most adorable, funniest person I know. She walks around like she owns the place. In our minds on some level, she does.

One issue that I was dwelling on was my attitude as a father. There is nothing like a mother's love. They can be the slightly more neurotic ones. It is a very fine line you have to toe as a dad, between trying to be the positive one and the one who is laid back but also respecting that there might be something to it. There might be something to your wife's paranoia and neuroses, so you say, "Okay, honey, let's check it out."

The Takeaway: Respect Your Spouse's (and Your Own) Parent Intuition

We are grateful for Feuerstein's willingness to walk us through the day he found out some of the most horrible news you can get. We all pray we'll never get a call like that. Hearing how it went for a fellow father and how he second-guessed his actions in hindsight was really powerful. It made us realize how many times we, as fathers, want to say "everything will be fine" or "don't overreact" to our significant others (or to that little voice in our heads), when really, what we should be saying is, "You may have a point. Let's check it out."

In a moment, your whole life can change—and that certainly made us appreciate all the "regular days" when nothing much happens.

Part III
Talents—What to Do Together

If Part I of this book is about your kids, and Part II is about you, then Part III is most definitely for both of you.

Want to teach your kid how to make a next-level Snoopy-inspired lunch? Or blast a soccer ball? Or get them into carpentry? Or learn how to exercise with you and have fun?

We got your back. This section shares tips on over two dozen activities and skills from a renowned group of dad experts, who have not only used their knowledge to teach their own kids but also to earn a living.

From three-time NBA Slam Dunk Contest champion Nate Robinson sharing exercises to help you both jump higher to celebrity chef Buddy Valastro on how to get kids into cooking to learning how to juggle and joggle (we'll explain) from Guinness World Record holder Michal Kapral, by the time you and your kids are done, you'll be the most talented father-kid duo on the block.

CHAPTER 10

Food

"If more of us valued food and cheer and song
above hoarded gold, it would be a merrier world."
—J.R.R. Tolkien, Father of Four

How to Get Your Kids to Try New Food
Buddy Valastro

DADOGRAPHY

Twitter: @CakeBossBuddy
Born: March 3, 1977
Kids: 4
Career: Master Chef, Bakery Owner

There are bosses…and then there are cake bosses. World famous baker Buddy Valastro is both. Valastro is the owner of Carlo's Bakery and the star of the reality TV show *Cake Boss*. He is a fourth-generation baker who began working for his father at the age of eleven. When he was seventeen and his father passed away, he took over Carlo's. Fifteen years later, his hit show debuted on TLC and put the family business (he works with his mom and four sisters) on the path to international culinary stardom.

Today, the Cake Boss brand includes TV shows, a wildly popular *YouTube* channel, more than a dozen locations of the bakery, a 55,000-square-foot, state-of-the-art baking facility in New Jersey, and several spin-off shows. Outside of business, Valastro has four kids who he preaches the value of family and hard work to. "We still make them do chores around the house," he says. "I take them to work with me. I make them earn a dollar. When they earn that dollar, they can spend that money just to understand about life. It is important in real life."

LOD: What is a great food to start baking with your kids, and how do you get them to try new things?

BV: Chocolate chip cookies. My kids started with cake decorating when they were younger but now they are on to cooking. I taught my son how to make pasta with broccoli the other day. My dad used to make it by putting anchovies in it. Now, you might think that kids wouldn't eat anchovies. He cooked with it. He tasted it. He was like, "Oh, man, this is really good."

It is always really hard to get kids to eat, but if they cook it, they almost feel like they have to eat it.

The Takeaway: Nothing Beats Hands-On Experience

When it comes to baking with kids, we love the idea of starting small with something like chocolate chip cookies. They have a low margin for error and very few ingredients. Also, if you haven't done a lot of baking, they're an easy starting point that have plenty of options for kids to get involved in: mixing, adding the chocolate chips, forming the cookies, etc.

Valastro's tip about anchovies is also spot on. It's so easy for kids to say they don't like a food or to give it a quick taste and spit it out. However, if they work with it, add it to other ingredients, and familiarize themselves with it, they're likely to look at it in a new light and give it a shot.

The Barbecue Strategy Your Kids Can Help With
Joe Horn

DADOGRAPHY

Twitter: @87JoeHorn
Born: January 16, 1972
Kid: Joe Jr.
Career: Entrepreneur, NFL Pro Bowler

There are unlikely roads to professional football stardom...and then there is the nearly impossible, barely-starting-anywhere-near-a-road path that former New Orleans Saints star Joe Horn traveled to reach the NFL. Horn played college football at tiny Itawamba Community College in Fulton, Mississippi, after which he worked at a Bojangles' Famous Chicken 'n Biscuits restaurant and didn't touch a football for almost two years. Down to his last few bucks, he went into a Blockbuster Video and got a tape of a Jerry Rice workout. He studied that workout, learned the drills, and created a football highlight tape that he sent to professional teams all over Canada and the United States. He heard from one: the Memphis Mad Dogs of the Canadian Football League (CFL).

After one successful year with Memphis, the United States arm of the CFL folded and Horn entered the NFL Draft, where the Kansas City Chiefs selected him in the fifth round. He played four seasons with Kansas City before signing with the New Orleans Saints and becoming a four-time Pro Bowler.

Now retired, Horn owns his own barbecue sauce company, Bayou 87, and spends time with his family.

LOD: What are some tips dads can use to grill the perfect meat with their kids?

JH: Let me give you a quick insight. Most people when they barbecue they take up to six or seven hours to prep the meat. Look, if you want a quick, prepped-up meat that tastes really good, probably tastes better than your average guy's barbeque, season your meat. Then cut it up and boil it. I know a lot of people say, "Joe, you are not supposed to boil up your meat." I say, "Whatever." Slather the meat in butter, then wrap up the meat in some tinfoil and put it in the oven. Cook it a little bit, like five, ten minutes. Take it out and throw it on the grill. You will have a quick barbecue that will taste better than the average guy who takes a day to marinate, cut, and prep his meat.

I had a barbecue cook-off with my uncle. He has been barbecuing for twenty-five years. We had a taste test, and I destroyed him. It took me an hour and fifteen minutes. It took him nine, ten hours to get his meat together and get ready. I boil the meat. I put it in the oven. I put some seasoning on it, then I put it up on the grill. It is easier, quicker, and everyone can eat faster.

The Takeaway: Lower the Steaks

One of the best parts about Horn's strategy for preparing the steak for a barbecue is that it's very kid-friendly, and most of the steps don't involve the fire, which we naturally keep kids away from. In fact, when you ask most dads about grilling for their family when they have younger kids, they'll admit the hardest part is keeping the kids away from the fire and hot grill.

Kids are naturally drawn to grilling, so with Horn's suggestion, you can take your kids to the grocery store or butcher shop to let them help you pick out the meat and then they can help you add the seasonings. Then all you need to do is throw the steak on the grill and, just like that, your kids are an integral part of the grilling process.

Make a Meal with Your Kids
Adam Perry Lang

DADOGRAPHY

Twitter: @AdamPerryLang
Kid: 1 daughter
Career: Chef, Restaurant Owner

Adam Perry Lang is a chef, restaurant owner, knife maker, *New York Times* bestselling author, fly fisherman, and family man. He has cooked at some of the finest restaurants in the world, including Daniel in New York City and Restaurant Guy Savoy in Paris, France. After earning his stripes on the world's culinary stage, Lang zeroed in on a food genre near and dear to his heart: barbecue.

As he worked his way through the world of smokers and brisket, he won Grand Champion Honors at the World Pork Expo and first place for pork shoulder at the "World Series of BBQ," aka, Kansas City's American Royal Invitational. He is the founder of Daisy May's BBQ in New York City, APL Restaurant in Hollywood, and many others.

LOD: You've shared pictures of your kid cooking with you, and it's clearly something you both enjoy. What are some tips you have for getting kids into cooking, and what's a great meal to make together?

APL: I will tell you something very interesting. My daughter has been cooking with me in the kitchen since age four. How do you involve a four-year-old? She is too young to handle a knife, so we prep together. Whenever I held the knife, she would hold my elbow. She would literally be at my side the whole time and hold my elbow. Getting your kids involved in cooking is one of the best things you can do.

She just recently used a steak knife. She is six years old and it is like she is a grownup. I don't encourage that with everybody, but I use my own knives. It is part of my culture of cooking. I have instilled a really deep respect for using them carefully.

One of the greatest things you can do is get kids to help you season. Teach them how to season like rain, which is really like sprinkling up high. Then get their hands full of olive oil and really rub the seasonings into the meat. Three things happen: They are doing something that grownups do, which they love. They are doing something with you, which they love. They are making a mess, which they love. So you got the trifecta right there.

I love to make pasta with them with flour and eggs. It is a heavy-duty activity. I like doing activities where they can really get involved. If it's just dumping spices in a bowl, that gets old quick. If you throw a big pile of flour, you got the eggs and they can mix the dough, it becomes a game. It gets rolled out, and they get so excited. At the end when they have seen that they created this pasta, which is one of their most favorite things in the world, it is like magic.

The Takeaway: Get Messy and Have Fun

This is some of the best cooking advice for kids we've seen from one of the best chefs in the world. Couple that with the idea that pasta and mac and cheese are usually at the top of most kids' favorite foods and you've got a recipe for family cooking success. If you want to go next level for the kids here, you can let each child create pasta in their favorite color. Here's how: once you've made the spaghetti (or whatever shape you've chosen), boil a few pots of water with your kids' favorite color using food coloring, and cook the pasta in those pots. This is great for Halloween, a birthday party, or to celebrate your favorite sports team.

Mastering the Lunch Box
Beau Coffron

DADOGRAPHY

Twitter: @lunchboxdad
Born: 1979
Kids: 3
Career: *Lunchbox Dad*

He's the Picasso of the cafeteria; the Da Vinci of deli meat; the Van Gogh of Go-Gurt. His real name is Beau Coffron, but to his tens of thousands of fans on social media, he's known as Lunchbox Dad. Give the man a few slices of bread, some ham, and some veggies, and he's liable to turn a kid's midday meal into a work of art that rivals anything in the Met. From Kermit the Frog to Minions to Snoopy to Snow White and hundreds of others, his character-themed lunchboxes are extraordinary.

His skills have landed him on *Good Morning America* and *The Steve Harvey Show*, and he's been featured in *HuffPost, Yahoo!, People* magazine, and others. He began making his next-level lunches when his oldest daughter was in kindergarten as a way to show her that he loved her and was thinking of her during the day. At first, he stuck with basic characters that she would enjoy and as she (and his other kids) have gotten older, he makes lunches with themes from his childhood, the 1980s, and other nostalgia he wants to introduce his children to. It's also a smart way to secretly introduce kids to new food because, as he says, if it looks fun, they're more likely to try it.

LOD: Your lunches are not only clever and creative but they're also very healthy and teach kids good habits about what a

complete meal can look like. What is a simple lunch dads can make with their kids if they're inspired by your work?

BC: Just start simple. If you have cookie cutters, just use them on sandwiches or pieces of cheese. Fresh fruits and vegetables are good to add color. There are things called vegetable cutters that are great to use on cucumbers and apples. Strawberries work out well and dried mango is good for shapes because it's usually flat. Tortillas work well too.

You can base what you make on what your kids are reading and what they're watching or what's happening in school. They can give you ideas, and you can work together on the lunches and what you want them to look like.

The Takeaway: Become the Lord of Lunches

Before you begin to make themed lunches for your kids, we highly encourage you to visit the *Lunchbox Dad* website (www.lunchboxdad .com) and *Instagram* feed to check out the level of artistry that he's operating on. We love what he's doing on so many levels, from making healthy meals for his kids to treating an empty lunchbox like a blank canvas. Show your kids the pictures of the lunches he has made and ask them what they'd like you to make. Then you can pick out the ingredients together and get to work on your culinary masterpiece.

And don't worry about adding twenty minutes to every morning to get this done. Saving your own legendary lunchbox for special occasions like birthdays works as well!

Playing the "Eat Vegetables Blindfolded" Game
Robert Irvine

DADOGRAPHY

Twitter: @RobertIrvine
Born: September 24, 1965
Kids: Annalise, Talia
Career: Chef, Restaurant Owner, TV Host

Chef Robert Irvine's path to culinary mastery began when he enlisted in the United Kingdom's Royal Navy at the age of fifteen. By age twenty-five, after ten years of service, he became an executive chef on luxury cruise ships and five-star restaurants. Capitalizing on his success and his increasing visibility in the celebrity chef universe, he began a career in TV by hosting *Dinner: Impossible* and *Kitchen: Impossible* on the Food Network.

Chef Irvine has since created a vast cooking and fitness empire that includes several books; the *Robert Irvine Magazine*; a line of healthy, high-protein foods called Fitcrunch; Gold's Gym ownership; speaking events; restaurants in both the Pentagon and Las Vegas; and a number of other achievements. Two of his favorite passions are supporting the military (he earned the Congressional Medal of Honor Society's Bob Hope Award for Excellence in Entertainment) and, of course, being a dad. He has two daughters in college who he still talks to "fifteen times a day" and works out with when he visits campus.

LOD: We all want to raise healthy kids, and the first step to making that happen is to teach them how to eat healthy. You've made fitness and nutrition a priority in your life and your family. Any tips to get kids to learn how to appreciate healthy foods?

RI: One thing I did with my girls was take them to the supermarket and let them pick out five green vegetables and five other vegetables of their own choosing—then we'd bring them back to the house. I'd let them taste each vegetable raw, then I would cook the product with them and then blindfold them and have them taste each dish, and I'd ask, "What's in this dish?"

For every one they got right, they got twenty-five cents. It would probably be a dollar these days, but it educates them about different flavors. The more you get kids in the kitchen and the more you have fun and make a mess, the better it is. When I work with both kids and adults I want them to have fun. That means making a mess. It means throwing flour at mom and dad in a playful way. Life is a sequence of moments we never get back. And the more fun moments they have in the kitchen, the better they retain the information.

The Takeaway: Forget the Hunger Games, How about the Veggie Games?

This is one of the best, most practical ideas we've heard for teaching kids how to eat right and to expand their palate. Not only does the vegetable taste test game involve kids picking out their own food, it involves hands-on cooking together, and it can be done on almost any budget and on any schedule. All you need is a blindfold, some veggies, and a quarter, and…let the games begin.

Quick tip: you can be a contestant in this game as well. Let your kids blindfold you, and join in on the fun. You'll laugh, and you'll get your veggies too.

CHAPTER 11

Sports and Fitness

"The principle is competing against yourself. It's about self-improvement, about being better than you were the day before."
—Steve Young, Father of Three

How to Have a Sweet Jump Shot
Dell Curry

DADOGRAPHY
Born: June 25, 1964
Kids: 3
Career: NBA Player, Basketball Analyst

He may be considered the "Father of Steph" to an entire generation of Golden State Warriors and NBA fans, but to basketball fans who grew up watching the game in the 1990s, Dell Curry built his own legacy as one of the smoothest shooters to ever lace up a pair of high tops. He also happened to play on one of the signature teams of the decade (the Charlotte Hornets) with two of the era's biggest stars (Larry Johnson and Alonzo Mourning).

Curry played for the Hornets for ten years, in addition to stints with the Toronto Raptors, the Milwaukee Bucks, and a few other teams. He won the NBA's Sixth Man of the Year Award in 1996 and at the age of thirty-four, he led the league in three-point shooting percentage. He's a career 40-percent shooter from behind the arc and is consistently mentioned whenever discussions arise about the player with the best-looking shot in NBA history. Fortunately for his sons, Steph and Seth, the apple didn't fall far from the tree. Both kids were born with natural shooting strokes, and thanks to Curry's early coaching, both sons have careers in the NBA (with Steph on the path to becoming an all-time great player and shooter).

LOD: We can only imagine the level of competition when it came to driveway shoot-arounds at your house when Steph and Seth were younger. What was your secret to developing a great jump shot?

DC: I tried to make five hundred shots a day. We shoot in practice and it wasn't really about how many you shot, but about how many you made. That is the bottom line. You want to make as many as you can. I always tried to set up a number and then try to reach that goal.

It was steady practice, and I was blessed with the ability to shoot a basketball. With that said, that skill was honed by putting in work every day. So on average I would try and make about five hundred shots per day.

The Takeaway: Practice Makes Perfect

We're not saying that if you follow Curry's advice, you'll immediately be able to drain ten-plus three-pointers in an NBA game, but when it comes to practicing hoops with your kids, choosing a number of made baskets for you both to reach and competing to see who gets there first is a great way to have some healthy competition. You can both rebound for each other, and as everyone who shoots hoops knows, the conversation flows the more shots you get up. It can be an awesome bonding experience.

Juggling (and Joggling) Tips
from a Guinness World Record Holder
Michal Kapral

DADOGRAPHY

Twitter: @mkapral
Born: 1972
Kids: 2
Career: Joggler, Guinness World Record Holder

Juggling is hard. Juggling while walking is harder. Juggling nonstop while running an entire marathon (aka joggling) should be nearly impossible. Not only must you have the physical stamina to run 26.2 miles and the ability to juggle the entire time, you must also possess the focus to block out the thousands of other runners on the route while keeping both your running and juggling rhythm. For Michal Kapral, the joggling world record holder in both the marathon and half-marathon, juggling while running for three hours is just a walk (er...run) in the park.

Kapral has completed the Boston, Chicago, Toronto, and New York City marathons while juggling, and he actually won the Toronto Marathon without juggling in 2002 with a time of 2:30:40. He has raised money for several charities throughout his joggling career and enjoys teaching kids, including his own, the joys of distance running. He has two daughters, and the next challenge he has set for himself is to run a 10k while juggling five balls, two more than the traditional three balls used in joggling.

LOD: You are considered the best in a sport that combines two very difficult tasks. What's the best way that dads and kids can learn to juggle and joggle together?

MK: The first thing is to set the expectation that you're going to be dropping the balls. Joggling can teach a great lesson about failure. If you drop a ball, you pick up and try again. The best way to start learning how to juggle three balls is to not even try to catch them. You can start out doing a pattern. One. Then two. Then you can do three. But the most important thing is to pay attention to where your tossing goes. The perfect toss will lead to the perfect catch.

It's just like if you're working on a three-point shot in basketball. At first, don't worry if the ball goes into the net. Focus on your form. Try tossing three balls in the air and seeing where they land. Then you don't have to worry about the frustration of dropping the balls. And then from there, it's just trying to do what we call a flash. One, two, three, and then catch all three of them. That's the first one. Then try to do four tosses. Then five tosses. And then you see how long you can go. It's a lesson in patience.

I've taught a whole bunch of kids how to juggle. Some kids get it faster than others. You just have to have the patience to keep trying. For the joggling part of it…every kid knows how to run. Once they've mastered juggling, the technique is similar, but you need to start moving and keep your juggling pattern close while not tossing the balls too far away from you.

The Takeaway: Get Joggle with It

Learning to juggle with your kids (or teaching them if you know how) is great because it's a fun, lifelong skill that will always please a crowd. The best part is all you need is some time and three tennis balls to get started. If you don't know how to juggle yet, it's a great activity to learn with your children because, as Kapral says, you'll both be dropping the balls all the time. You can take the opportunity to teach your kids how to laugh at themselves, how to have patience, and how to fight through failure.

In the end, you'll both have a cool party skill (and if you think you can juggle for 26.2 miles in under two hours and forty minutes, maybe a Guinness World Record!).

Master the Basics of Kicking a Soccer Ball
Jeff Attinella

> **DADOGRAPHY**
>
> Twitter: @Jeff_Attinella1
> Born: September 29, 1988
> Kid: Remy
> Career: Professional Soccer Goalie, Author

As far as professional athletes with side hustles, Portland Timbers goalkeeper Jeff Attinella's off-season job as children's book author is one of the more unique (and best) pairings we've seen. When he's not leading his Timbers to the Major League Soccer playoffs, the University of Southern California grad is writing books about the championship sports teams for his It Had to Be Told book series.

The series itself was inspired by his love of sports and the birth of his daughter, Remy. When Remy was born, Attinella was looking for a way to share with her the same bonding experiences over sports that he had with his dad, and he settled on the idea of a book series. "This way, parents can read with their kids and bond over their favorite sports experiences," he says. So far, the book series includes books such as *The Curse Ends*, which covers the Chicago Cubs' historic 2016 season; *Roll, Crimson, Roll*, about University of Alabama football; and *Cleveland Wins a Championship,* about the 2016 Cleveland Cavaliers.

LOD: It seems like a rite of passage for most kids to play at least one soccer season in their lives. What are some fun drills and games dads can play with their kids to help them improve while also having fun?

JA: There's a great game called soccer tennis, where you set up a net and the rules are kind of like volleyball except you're not allowed to use your hands. The idea for little kids is to learn to position their feet so they can kick the ball in the air. They learn how to control the ball, how to pass it over the net, how to control the weight they put behind the ball, and where they kick it.

As for the perfect placement to get your foot on the ball's sweet spot, you want to teach kids to strike the ball with the hard bone on the inside of your foot, where the big toe connects to the rest of your foot. You're looking for them to make contact and drive through the ball.

The most important thing with kids is working on having their shoulders, hips, and follow-through in line with their target. A good way to practice is to point out where you insert the needle into the ball and use that as your target area and work on hitting that spot with the hard area of your foot.

The Takeaway: Setting Goals to Score Goals

Little kid soccer matches tend to devolve quickly into a scrum of kids running around chaotically, half chasing the ball and half chasing each other. Attinella's idea to turn soccer into a smaller version of itself, with a volleyball-like feel, is perfect for any dad who wants to help his kid practice in a fun way in the backyard. With you on one side of the net and your child on the other, you can help them work on their form as they kick it over the net (or a row of cones or a towel on the ground) while you then demonstrate the form as you kick it back.

How to Add Inches to Your Vertical and Teach Competition

Nate Robinson

DADOGRAPHY

Twitter: @Nate_Robinson
Born: May 31, 1984
Kids: Navyi, Nahmier, Ny'ale, Nasir
Career: NBA Slam Dunk Champion, Entrepreneur

The average adult man in the United States stands 5'9" tall. The average height for an NBA player is 6'7". From a mathematical standpoint alone, 5'8" Nate Robinson has no business being in the NBA, let alone winning the league's famous dunk contest three times against stars like Dwight Howard and Andre Iguodala. And yet, that's exactly what Robinson did in addition to putting up some excellent numbers with the New York Knicks and being a key role player on the Boston Celtics 2010 NBA Finals team.

Robinson was Mr. Basketball *and* Mr. Football his senior year in high school in Seattle and he played both sports his freshman year at the University of Washington. While he's been blessed with speed and explosive quickness, he talks about jumping high with a passion the way artists talk about their craft. He has four kids, the oldest ones already making a name for themselves on the court. Robinson is often on the sidelines cheering with a giant smile on his face.

LOD: Your kids are following in your footsteps as athletes, which clearly makes you proud. For dads who want to help their kids jump higher or improve at basketball while maybe getting a little better themselves, what workouts do you recommend?

NR: I've been putting a ball in my kids' hands since before they could walk. Once they could start to dribble, I would have them copy me. I'd just have them dribble behind me with one hand while we walked around the three-point line, then we'd dribble with the other hand the other way. Or we'd count dribbles. Ten right. Ten left. The most important thing is for the ball to begin to feel like it's part of them, or you. Shooting is about volume in the beginning. You have to get your shots up, then work on form. But not just shots. Real jump shots.

One game I play with my kids is I'll pick a spot on the court and see how many jump shots I can make in a row. I try to put a big number up there, and then they have to try to match me. It's competitive and we have fun. My daughter picked up my work ethic, and she'll be out there now shooting jumpers by herself. Her passion for my passion, basketball, is overwhelming. Almost brings a tear to my eye. She can hoop!

When it comes to jumping, that's about being explosive. A cool game is to find something like a spot on the backboard or the goalpost just out of reach and you each try to jump and touch it ten times. You can do it next to each other. Practice swinging your arms up into every jump. Then do the same thing, just using your legs and holding a ball above your head. You can have a regulation-sized ball and your kid can have a kid's ball. If you do that a few times a week, you'll improve both leg strength and vertical quickly.

The Takeaway: It's Fun Being the Pops with Hops

While all of the exercises and drills Robinson mentions are fun for you and your kids, we know that most of you reading this won't end up dunking on a 10-foot hoop. But don't let that stop you from showing off the improved vertical that you and your kids have built up by working out together. After you've got your jump shots up, remember to drop your driveway or middle school hoop down to six or eight feet for some rim-rocking fun. Throwing down a nasty reverse on a 7-foot hoop can feel every bit as exhilarating as if it was done on a 10-foot version.

Smart Rules for Teaching Tennis to Kids
James Blake

DADOGRAPHY

Twitter: @JRBlake
Born: December 28, 1979
Kids: Riley, Emma
Career: Tennis Analyst, Tennis Star

Despite winning ten singles titles and seven doubles titles on the ATP tour, James Blake's signature tennis match was likely his epic face-off with Andre Agassi in the quarterfinals of the 2005 US Open. After defeating Rafael Nadal in an earlier round, Blake went toe-to-toe with Agassi for several hours on one of the sport's most famous courts, which was only an hour from where Blake grew up. With both men exhausted, Agassi ultimately won in a fifth set tiebreak, after which the legend said, "I wasn't the winner, tennis was."

If you talk to Blake (and from what he told us, his mom too), the proudest moment of his tennis career actually occurred away from the court, when he won the Arthur Ashe Humanitarian of the Year Award in 2008. Blake grew up worshipping Ashe and says the more he learned about him as he grew up, the more he wanted to be like him as a player and as a man. Blake is now retired and has two young daughters who he recently began introducing to the sport.

LOD: Now that your own daughters are old enough to pick up rackets and get on the court with you, what are some games you play with them to keep tennis fun and to teach them the fundamentals?

JB: The first thing is that kids want to have fun. If there's one thing they love to do on the court, then you can just do that. If they love hitting forehands all day, then just do that and add in two minutes of hitting a backhand. For my daughters, the biggest thing for me is to keep them active.

You don't want to teach footwork or anything yet, that's too advanced. But what you can do in general is to have them moving their feet. What I like to do is have them do anything where they hit the ball and then run around the net or hit the ball and then run back to the line. All things to keep them moving, and it's also good for tiring them out so they sleep at night. It's good to teach them that tennis is not a sport where you just sit still and walk to the back of the line.

Some other basic stuff to teach them is what's called "sit and lift," where you bend down a little and lift straight up. The racket goes up, and they hit through the ball. The main key for parents and coaches is to not get frustrated with your kids. If they're done after fifteen minutes, then that's fine. Maybe next time it'll be twenty minutes.

The Takeaway: Keep 'Em Moving

We live in an age of out-of-control coaches and parents who truly think their six-year-old is going to be a professional athlete...so it's nice to hear a former pro athlete say the most important thing for kids to learn at a young age is that the sport they're playing is fun. For those of us who have taken our kids to a tennis court, the games Blake mentioned are a godsend. The hardest part about teaching young kids any activity is the downtime. Having games where kids hit the ball and then run around the net or run to the back line or even do some jumping jacks is a great way to minimize the "standing around" time and maximize the fun (and active) times.

The Key to Teaching Your Kids How to Hit a Baseball or Softball
Felipe Alou

DADOGRAPHY

Born: May 12, 1935
Kids: Moisés, Maria, Jennifer, Christia, Cheri, Valerie
Career: MLB Manager, Baseball Legend

In terms of sheer baseball knowledge, it would be nearly impossible to top Felipe Alou in particular and the Alou family in general. Felipe was one of three brothers who made it to the major leagues in the 1960s, and he was one of the first Dominican athletes to become an everyday player. Over the course of his sixteen-year career (which spanned six different teams), he became friends with baseball giants like Roberto Clemente (of the Pittsburgh Pirates) and played alongside actual (New York) Giants, like Willie Mays and Willie McCovey. He made three All-Star teams before retiring to become a hitting coach in 1974.

In 1992, he became the manager of the Montreal Expos, where he would get the opportunity to coach one of his sons, All-Star outfielder Moisés Alou. He won National League Manager of the Year in 1994. Following the baseball strike in 1994, team management held a fire sale, getting rid of all the best players. Alou hung on for a few more years before ultimately winding up back in San Francisco as their new manager in 2001, where he coached until 2006 before moving to the front office.

LOD: You were an excellent baseball player, just like your brothers and son. So many of the dads reading have sons and daughters playing baseball or softball. What is one piece of advice you could give them when it comes to hitting?

FA: At all levels, the better hitters have to hit fastballs. You have to teach your kids to hit fastballs. My brothers and I were all different sizes, but we had one thing in common—all three of us could hit a fastball. The fastball is going to be the pitch that closes the game. Every time I'd go around the minor leagues when I worked with the Giants, I would ask, "Are you a good fastball hitter?" They'd say they were, but then I'd ask, "How many fastballs can you hit well if you get ten fastballs," and then you'd have your answer.

You are always going to get fastballs, so you have to be able to hit them. Strikeouts and fly balls kill hitters. Line drives and ground balls keep hitters alive. When I was managing, I'd say, "I can't manage fly balls or strikeouts." Ground balls, you can do things. You can move runners. You can get a bad throw. A lot can happen. I believe that children have to be taught early to not miss fastballs. Teach them when they're young. You can get away with being a bad breaking ball hitter as long as you can hit fastballs.

The Takeaway: Learn to Hit the Heater

Every father reading this involved with kids who play junior high baseball and softball knows the tendency coaches have to teach kids how to hit curveballs, despite the fact that few high school pitchers can regularly throw curveballs for strikes.

The best part about Alou's advice is that you can make it into a fun activity to do with your kids. Go with your kids to batting cages, get in the cage next to them, and have fastball-hitting contests. You can head into a cage with a slower pitch (if you need to), your son or daughter can swing at a higher velocity, and you can chart how many you each hit well. Give two points for a line drive, one point for a solid ground ball, and zero points for pop-ups or dribblers. Game on.

Smart Ways to Exercise with Your Kids
Gunnar Peterson

DADOGRAPHY

Twitter: @Gunnar
Born: 1965
Kids: 4
Career: Trainer, NBA Director of Strength and Endurance

It's easy to introduce personal trainer Gunnar Peterson by the A-list celebrities and the championship athletes he has worked with. He's helped Sly Stallone rebuild his *Rocky* and *Expendables* physique. He's helped Jennifer Lopez stay in peak condition. He's worked with Angelina Jolie, Sofía Vergara, and the Kardashians and now he's the director of strength and endurance training for the Los Angeles Lakers.

Peterson has trained athletes in nearly every major sport, many of them in his own private gym in Los Angeles. He's made regular contributions to *Men's Health* and *Muscle & Fitness* and a variety of talk shows…and don't get him started on his fury about the so-called "dad bod." On that note, he has four kids, and when he talked to us about strength training and exercise, he spoke personally about his desire to "never be on the sidelines" with his own kids. His reasons for staying in shape and eating right center around his desire to be as active and engaged with his kids as he can.

LOD: What are some strategies dads can use to get exercise for themselves while also playing with their kids and teaching them the basics of working out and living a healthy lifestyle?

GP: Kids can do push-ups, body weight squats, pull-ups, rear lunges, mountain climbers, all those kinds of things. There are some studies out there that overhead work can cause some problems, so just don't overhead press, and you're good. Also, don't push them to lift as much as they possibly can. All basic common-sense stuff. A good idea is to have your kid work out with you but use a dowel while you're using a barbell.

You've got to Tom Sawyer it with kids. You're painting the fence. Don't tell them to paint the fence, because they're going to resist. You paint the fence and make it look like a lot of fun and then slowly allow them to do a little bit of the painting with you. Then they're engaged on their own volition and you didn't make them do it. There are so many things vying for their free time. Your routine has to be fun. You can play with them and have them hold their Hot Wheels while you use weights. Incorporate their toys into your movements and it becomes fun for them. If they're riding their Big Wheels in the backyard, you run to one point and have them bike to you, then have them get off and push the thing.

The Takeaway: Toying Around in the Gym

Peterson provided some fantastic, actionable advice throughout our interview, but we especially like the idea of incorporating your kids' toys into a workout that they'll enjoy. You probably won't have much success trying to teach an eight-year-old form for a power clean or deadlift, but you will have success letting them copy you while they use a Wiffle ball bat and you use a barbell.

And above all else, make it fun. If your son or daughter doesn't like being in the gym, ride intervals on your bikes or run grassy hills near your house and then roll down together.

Thoughts on Kids Playing Football
Chad Pennington

DADOGRAPHY

Twitter: @ChadPennington
Born: June 26, 1976
Kids: 3
Career: NFL Quarterback, Businessman

When Chad Pennington retired from the NFL, he had the highest career completion percentage for a quarterback in the league's history (at 66 percent), while also throwing for 102 touchdowns. He also won the NFL's Comeback Player of the Year Award two times, which nobody else had ever done. In his eleven years of professional football, split between the New York Jets and Miami Dolphins, Pennington earned a reputation as an accurate passer, an excellent teammate, and a great leader.

Pennington's current focus is on the 1st and 10 Foundation that he established with his wife. The organization was created to build stronger communities by funding programs to help improve the quality of life in areas important to the Penningtons, including eastern Tennessee, southern West Virginia, and the tri-state area. Since it was founded in 2003, they have donated over $1 million to various local causes. When not raising money, Pennington is raising his three boys, who are following in his footsteps with a passion for sports.

LOD: You won the William V. Campbell Trophy in college, often referred to as the "Academic Heisman." You also have three boys. What are your thoughts on the future of football and what do you tell dads who ask you if they should let their sons play?

CP: We certainly believe in all the positive things that surround the game of football and what it teaches our young men. There is mental toughness, physical toughness, teamwork, and accountability. You have to take ownership for your actions. We believe in those things that football provides.

We also think that there is an older age—whether it be fifth, sixth, seventh, or eighth grade, the parent can decide—where it is appropriate for a child to play tackle. Any time before that, I think flag football is more appropriate. Number one, they learn more. They learn hand-eye coordination and they are aware of their surroundings. They don't have to worry about contact.

Secondly, if they love the game but are not ready for contact, you don't want to take the game away from them. We think that whenever they are ready, they will know. There are so many positive things that come out of football. Are we worried about the injury risk? Yes. If you look at specialization of baseball and soccer and those types of sports, there are kids out there who have Tommy John surgery and who are tearing their ACLs at twelve and thirteen years old because they are playing too much. You've got to make sure that you are giving your kids a break. You should teach them properly how to play the game. Give them a mental and physical break. They don't need to play the same sport all year round.

The Takeaway: The Choice Is Yours

Specializing in one particular sport has become an unhealthy, yet very popular, craze among parents. Quick reminder: your children are living out their own athletic careers, not the dreams you once had for yourself. Since it is likely your son isn't the next LeBron James or Aaron Rogers and your daughter isn't the next Sue Bird or Serena Williams, having them play just one sport when they're young makes no sense. Expose them to as many sports as they're interested in, and let them make the choice.

As for whether or not your boys should play football, that is a personal choice that you can think about with your child, your partner, and/or your child's pediatrician.

Sharing History
Ken Griffey Sr.

DADOGRAPHY

Born: April 10, 1950
Kids: 2
Career: MLB Player

Whether he is more famous in sports circles as the father of "The Kid" or for his own extraordinary baseball exploits, Ken Griffey Sr. left his mark on Major League Baseball. He won two World Series rings as a member of Cincinnati's famous "Big Red Machine" and made the All-Star Game three times during his eight years with the Reds. He also won the All-Star Game MVP in 1980.

One of the most memorable moments of his life, however, combined both his sports career and his life as a parent. It took place on September 14, 1990, when he played in a professional game for the Seattle Mariners with his son, Ken Griffey Jr., and they did something that seemed impossible: hit back-to-back, father-son home runs. At the time, Griffey Sr. was forty years old and Griffey Sr. was twenty. No father and son duo had ever hit back-to-back home runs in the history of Major League Baseball.

LOD: You were part of one of the most famous father-son feats in sports history. Can you take us inside the experience of hitting back-to-back home runs with your son as a father?

KG: We first went on the field together on August 31, 1990. Getting the opportunity to play with Junior was the highlight of my career. As for that day, I remember Harold (Reynolds) being on first base. I hit a home run to left-center field. As I am rounding third heading home, the first person who is going to meet me is Junior. Looking into his eyes, I see a difference in him. It was a transition. I knew his concentration level was sky high. After he gave me a high five, he got in the batter's box.

Harold Reynolds and I were talking on our way back to the dugout. He says, "You know, if he hits a home run, it will be the first time a father and son ever did it."

I didn't think of it that way. I guess Harold and Junior had been talking about it. When he went to 3-0, I didn't think he would have a chance. He hit a fastball or a sinker low and away. He hit it to left-center field. Dante Bichette in left field was like, "You gotta be kidding."

It was an amazing night for both of us. When he got to home plate he was looking for me the whole time. He was grinning from ear to ear. That was such a fun time and he was just grinning at me. He gave me a big hug. I was thinking, "Oh my God, he did it." All the pressure was on him. He was a stud. He was the man.

The Takeaway: Make Your Own History with Your Kids

Since hitting back-to-back home runs in Major League Baseball by a father and son hadn't happened before and hasn't happened since, we can lower the bar a little bit and not hold ourselves to that exact standard of father-son achievement. However, we can keep our eyes open for achievements that we can share with our kids.

Whether it's running a 5k together or completing a hiking trail or even learning a song on an instrument together, pay attention to common interests that you have with your kids and come up with goals together. Your pinnacle might not be back-to-back home runs in a Major League stadium, but the two of you crossing a finish line together is equally cool.

CHAPTER 12

Entertainment and Skills

"Creativity is putting your imagination to work, and it's produced the
most extraordinary results in human culture."
—Ken Robinson, Father of Two

Best Video Games for Dads and Daughters
Tony Hawk

DADOGRAPHY

Twitter: @TonyHawk
Born: May 12, 1968
Kids: Riley, Keegan, Spencer, Kadence
Career: Skateboarder, Entrepreneur

Tony Hawk became a professional skateboarder at fourteen years old
and won his first contest in 1983, back in his sport's relative infancy.
By the time he was eighteen, he'd won dozens of contests and was on
his way to revolutionizing the entire world of skateboarding, culminating in his being the first athlete to ever land a 900, which is a trick
with the absolute highest level of difficulty that involves spinning
two-and-a-half times in the air before landing.

He's also appeared as himself in several movies and TV shows. His video game series, including the iconic *Tony Hawk's Pro Skater, Tony Hawk: Motion*, and *Tony Hawk: Shred*, are among the bestselling action sports video games of all time. As perhaps a cherry on top of his skating career, he was invited to the White House in 2009 by President Obama and was given official clearance to skate on the grounds…a far cry from the days of skating in empty backyard pools in Southern California.

Hawk has four kids, spanning sixteen years, so he's handling the adult child situation while also helping his daughter navigate elementary school.

LOD: For many young fans, your skateboarding accomplishments may be second in popularity to your video games. How did your son Riley end up in one of your games and what games do you play with your daughter?

TH: The request came from the fans of the game. It didn't come from me personally. I have watched him over the years shy away from projects I have been involved with because he wants to carve his own path. I have to respect that. So I was a little hesitant to even ask him. I didn't want him to be uncomfortable about it. He was immediately on board. I was thankful that he appreciates the game enough to be included on it even though it has my name on it.

I have been playing a lot of Mario with my daughter. We just got a Wii U. That has been her introduction into video games. She really, really loves it. Actually, last night we were playing Super Smash Bros. until bedtime. She destroyed me on our last three battles. I was trying. It is not funny anymore. I am not letting her win.

The Takeaway: Video Games Are All about Bonding

Two dreams most kids have who play video games are 1) being able to one day play themselves in the game and 2) when they grow up, playing games with their kids. The dynamic in the Hawk household is slightly different, considering the family name is the game and Tony Hawk, aka Dad, is the star of the game. Gaming is a huge part of Hawk's legacy, and it's fantastic that he's passed that on to his daughter as well and is playing games that she'll enjoy. Mario is the perfect starter-level game for kids (although take it from Hawk, losing is never fun, even if it's to your daughter).

How to Raise an Avid Reader
Steve Rushin

DADOGRAPHY

Twitter: @SteveRushin
Born: September 22, 1966
Kids: 4
Career: Author, Sportswriter

While some writers can say they've traveled far and wide for their craft, few can say that they've traveled as far as Steve Rushin, who has filed stories from Greenland, India, and the icing on the travel cake, Antarctica, where he profiled swimsuit model Kate Upton's photo shoot. Rushin has long been a staple at *Sports Illustrated* and has written for *Time* and *Golf Digest* as well.

He has published several books, including the novel *The Pint Man* and his most recent, critically acclaimed memoir, *Sting-Ray Afternoons*. When he's not writing (which, as a work-from-home dad, only takes place between 8 a.m. and 3 p.m.), he's shuffling his four kids to practices and games. He is also the cohost of the *Ball & Chain Podcast* with his wife, Pro Basketball Hall of Famer and WNBA legend Rebecca Lobo.

LOD: As a writer, author, wordsmith, and father, you're on the front lines of the battle to make sure kids put down the technology and read a book. What strategies have worked for you with your kids to pass down the skill to focus and enjoy reading and writing?

SR: We're blessed to have a house full of books, and our kids love to read. And I read every night with my ten-year-old son. He stacks up his books and it's like a bar graph of our reading achievements. He puts them on his shelf and it's like a trophy case of the books that he's read. Our twelve-year-old daughter and our oldest one now love to read on their own. They see me writing, and one time, my son asked to use my laptop and I thought he was on Nick Jr. or something. He closed it when I walked up to him…but later I found a file he had written with a short, six-paragraph story on Jackie Robinson that moved me to tears. Our eight-year-old is now writing stories. Kids are so unfettered. They write in a way that there are no rules. I encourage it.

The Takeaway: Treat Finishing a Book the Same As Athletic Accomplishments

We think nothing of handing our kids a trophy after a soccer season or giving them a ribbon for competing in a tournament. The reason we do those things is to encourage further participation in that activity. Often, we treat reading like a chore or homework, when it can and should be so much more.

Rather than only reading assigned books from school or the latest middle grade sensation, find books that are specific to things your kids like and bring those books home for you to read together. And rather than putting finished books in a drawer or on a desk, follow Rushin's lead and use a special bookshelf reserved for books that your child has read start to finish. Create your own book club, with rewards for five books, ten books, and beyond.

How You and Your Kids Can Take Perfect Photos
Ian Spanier

DADOGRAPHY

Twitter: @IanSpanierPhoto
Born: March 13, 1974
Kids: 2 sons
Career: Photographer

From celebrity portraits of mainstream actors to action shots on the side of cliffs to up-close and personal photos of UFC stars, boxers, and MVPs of the major professional sports, photographer Ian Spanier has traveled the globe snapping pictures of the biggest names for the largest publications. He's brought his camera weightlifting with The Rock, in the gym with Dave Batista, and even into the ocean with Navy SEALS. Through it all, Spanier aims to capture the perfect shot of his subjects.

In addition to this work with athletes and entertainers, Spanier has published several photography books, including *Playboy: The Book of Cigars* and *Local Heroes: Portraits of American Volunteer Firefighters*. He's also a lecturer for many photography companies and the Fashion Institute of Technology in New York City. He lives in Los Angeles, has two boys, and admits to getting roped into helping out on their school picture day.

LOD: With every phone having a camera and apps having multiple filters, everyone thinks they're on the verge of being a professional photographer. Kids also love taking pictures now since it's so easy. What are some tips for parents and kids to properly capture moments and events?

IS: The number one most important thing for making good images is lighting. You don't need to be an expert in lighting, but paying attention to where the sun is and when it looks best is important. If you want to take great pictures with your kids, and of them, take them outside at the beginning of the day and end of the day for the best light.

As for perspective, if you're taking photos of your kids, get on your knees or sit down so you're at their eye level for a favorable angle. And the same goes in reverse for when your kids are shooting you. Have them stand on a chair or a car bumper so they're close to eye-to-eye.

If you're letting your kids take pictures with your phone, the most important thing is to get out of the default wide angle. So when you hit the camera icon on your phone, zoom in halfway and then hand your phone to your kids. Have them use their feet to adjust distance, rather than the zoom.

If your child is really enjoying photography and you want them to learn more, get them a basic point-and-shoot 35mm camera. I got my first one when I was six and I took photos of everything. Take them outside to great places in nature and let them shoot you with all kinds of cool backgrounds. They'll have a blast.

The Takeaway: Point, Shoot, and Have Fun

There isn't a parent alive in the modern age of smartphones with cameras whose little kids don't become obsessed with taking pictures at some point. Rather than have them eat up your storage space with a bunch of blurry images and cut-off headshots in your kitchen, walk them through the basics of Spanier's tips and then follow his other advice and head to a park for a mock photo shoot. You're sure to end up with some awesome pictures (and in the era of posting family photos on *Instagram* and *Facebook*, having some fundamental photography skills isn't the worst thing in the world).

How to Make Learning an Instrument Enjoyable for You and Your Kids
Siddhartha Khosla

DADOGRAPHY

Twitter: @SiddKhoslaMusic
Born: January 2, 1977
Kids: 3
Career: Musician, Composer

If you (or your spouse) are one of the millions of Americans who get slightly weepy every Tuesday night watching the juggernaut TV series *This Is Us*, then show composer Siddhartha Khosla is partly to blame for your weekly rendezvous with your emotions. Khosla, whose *This Is Us* original score debuted at the top of the iTunes soundtrack chart, has composed the music for all three seasons of the show, winning several awards. He also scores the music for *The Kids Are Alright* and Marvel's *Runaways*.

When he's not making music for hit shows, he is the songwriter and singer for his critically acclaimed band Goldspot. Khosla, along with his band, were invited to perform at the White House in 2013 by Michelle Obama as the musical guests for the Diwali festival. Khosla plays a variety of instruments and is famous for the eclectic instruments he works into his music, including the Greek bouzouki and the Flemish harpsichord. When he's home, however, the music he's likely to be hearing is a real-life soundtrack of kids running around and laughing and crying because he has three kids five years old and under.

LOD: Many dads have "learn an instrument" on their bucket list while also wanting their kids to learn the guitar or piano. What are some tips for parents who want to learn an instrument with their kids?

SK: I've been going through this with my own five-year-old and there's a little bit of a tiger parent thing that can happen. You don't want to force your kid to play. You want to see if they like music on their own. The most important thing is giving kids access to the instrument. If you have space in your house, make a music nook so they have a place to play. A space dedicated to music will draw them in. You can get a used guitar from Guitar Center and have it there so kids see it every day —that makes a big difference.

Another way to build excitement around the learning is to learn songs together that they like or you like. My kids still listen to Katy Perry's "Roar" over and over. If your daughter loves Katy Perry, but doesn't like practicing other songs, you can have the instructor teach her a Katy Perry song. I listen to the Beatles in the car and now my daughter wants to learn "Hey Jude." And so she'll practice that. All these pop songs are often very simple musically. For the verses of "Hey Jude" it's two verses over and over again. That's easy for both of you to learn.

The Takeaway: Play Music That Kids Want to Listen To

For those of us who were forced to take music lessons when we were younger, one of the most difficult parts of starting out is how boring the music is that you have to play. Khosla's tips about learning music that you and your kids actually like is extremely important because the payoff of playing songs you enjoy is closer. Also, having a dedicated place for music, even if it's in the corner of a room or a garage, lends itself to creativity and provides you and your kids a place to rock out any time you want.

Build Practical Things with Your Kids
Adam Carolla

> **DADOGRAPHY**
>
> Twitter: @AdamCarolla
> Born: May 27, 1964
> Kids: Natalia, Santino "Sonny"
> Career: Comedian, Author, TV Host, Director, Radio Personality, Guinness World Record Holder

Prior to starting the world's most downloaded podcast (*The Adam Carolla Show*) and before appearing on one of the longest-running, most popular syndicated radio shows with Dr. Drew (*Loveline*), and before his run on Comedy Central's *The Man Show*, Adam Carolla was a man who first and foremost enjoyed working with his hands. Whether as a boxer, a carpenter, or a mechanic, when he wasn't working behind a microphone or in front of a camera, Carolla typically had several projects in some phase of construction.

As he's built his media empire, he's incorporated more of his passion into his programming, with offerings like *The Car Show* and

Catch a Contractor. He's also written two *New York Times* bestselling books and is raising twins (one boy, one girl) with his wife. Like so many dads, Carolla is working hard to give his kids an appreciation for nondigital skills that involve time away from smartphones and flat screens.

LOD: As a man who has worked construction jobs and who has legitimate carpentry skills, what strategies or projects have you used to teach your kids the value of being able to build things with their own two hands?

AC: Kids now are digital people. They're not mechanical people. Everything in their world involves a computer, a screen, chips, and technology. They're not "manual shift" or "change your own oil" people. If you try and build something that's less useful for them, like a hummingbird feeder, I don't know if they'll want to do that.

I recently built my daughter a platform for her bed. And I built my son a loft for his bedroom. So I built them a couple of things that went in their rooms that they slept on. If you want to build a project that ends up in their room (like a bed or desk or loft) or something that they will use, then there might be a little more skin in the game. I still did all the work myself, but I did get my son out there to help me build the ladder. And we went to Home Depot while I bought the materials and it felt like we were doing it together.

The Takeaway: Have Your Kids Help Build Their Own Room

Every single parent we've talked to struggles with the effect too much tech will have on their kids—and we all do our best to introduce skills and projects that don't involve screen time. While hands-on construction projects are excellent to teach real-life skills, teamwork, and focus to our kids (and are a lot of fun to work on together), Carolla makes a great point. How interested is your son or daughter really going to be in constructing a birdfeeder or stool that sits in a closet most of the time? But if you take on a project that will end up in their rooms, that they see and use every day, they'll have a greater appreciation for the work that goes into it and for you taking the time to build it with them. Choose something that's within your own skill level and involve them in as much of the project as possible.

Teaching Kids How to Visualize and Achieve Goals
Tim Allen

DADOGRAPHY

Twitter: @ofcTimAllen
Born: June 13, 1953
Kids: Elizabeth, Katherine
Career: Comedian, Actor, Voice Actor

Between Tim Allen's hit sitcoms *Home Improvement* and *Last Man Standing*, he has played a father on TV for sixteen years and has raised six TV kids. In that span, he's been nominated for five Golden Globe Awards and one Emmy (winning the award in 1995 for his role as Tim "The Tool Man" Taylor). He has also played St. Nick himself in all three *The Santa Clause* movies and he has been famously voicing Buzz Lightyear for more than twenty years in the legendary *Toy Story* movies.

Allen grew up outside of Detroit, Michigan, and although he has had incredible success as an actor in TV and film, his career in show business began as a stand-up comedian. In fact, his first time on stage was the result of a dare. After moving to Los Angeles, he became a recurring comedian at the world-famous club The Comedy Store, which led to late-night talk show appearances and ultimately TV roles. Allen has two grown daughters.

LOD: One thing about being a father is that children share goals with you that may seem outrageous. As a stand-up comedian, you went from open mic nights in Detroit to major movie franchises. What is the biggest goal of yours that you achieved throughout your career, and how did you go about reaching it?

TA: Doing The Tonight Show *with Johnny Carson was my goal. I have a picture of it up right here in my office. I have had a lot of trouble in my life focusing myself. And I never really thought about it until I read some self-help books and motivational books by men and women who did things that I loved. But they weren't me. I realized early on that if you focus and set goals, you can achieve goals. Small goals. Large goals. They're all the same format. You have to focus and do the work. If you do the work, you can get the goal.*

When I first started thinking about being on The Tonight Show, *it looked impossible from where I was. And then my focus got me there, and that set up so many other things. Then Johnny called me over to his desk, which signaled that I was funny. So many things up to that point were because of focus, and so many things after that were because of focus.*

The Takeaway: Focus Equals Success

We saved this entry for last in this section because it applies not only to all of the skills in this last third of the book but because it applies to any large goals your kids may want to set. Oftentimes as parents, we hear our kids say things like, "I want to be a rock star!" or "I want to be an astronaut" or countless other professions that seem difficult to achieve. Too frequently, we dismiss it or say we'll talk about it later. But following Tim Allen's lead, what if we teach our kids to focus and take that goal one step at a time, who knows what will happen?

For the child who wants to be a rock star, have them focus on an instrument. Then have them focus on one song, then another more difficult song. Let the experience guide them where they want to go. Or if they want to be a chef, have them focus on one recipe first, rather than saying becoming a chef seems impossible. Start small. Focus. Help your child set reasonable goals. Then you can both enjoy the journey to success.

Conclusion

Our goal for this project was simple: to write the most useful, entertaining, all-encompassing book of fatherhood advice and thoughts ever assembled, from the most wide-ranging, iconic group of dads we could talk to. We hope the overriding takeaway is that it doesn't matter if you're a billionaire, a Grammy winner, an Emmy winner, a Hall of Famer, an entrepreneur, an astronaut, an office worker, a boss, or an employee—when it comes to responsibilities, we all have the same job, and it's the most important one: being the best dad we can be.

Index